I0480374

# Martha and the Maids of the Square Table

*A very human take on Leadership (with a goose)*

Dale Gunstone

Published by 'designed by dannii publishing'
www.designedbydannii.my.canva.site/


Paperback ISBN: 978-1-9192643-9-4

# DEDICATION

This book is dedicated to the many National Westminster Bank tutors I had the privilege of working alongside during my time at the Group Training Centre, Skills Development Centre, London Development Centre and Heythrop Park.

There are far too many people to name individually, but some rightly stand out for the belief they placed in me, the support they offered while shaping my development as a trainer, and the encouragement they continued to give long after our working paths diverged. This dedication is also for those we have sadly lost along the way. You are remembered always and remain forever in my heart.

With gratitude and affection, I dedicate this book to:

Roger, Sandra, Karen, Lynn, Dawn, Julie, Lisa, Melina, Sharon, Liz, Jeni, KLF, Alastair, Tim, Helen, Keith, Ian, Charles, Phyllida, Dianne, Jane, Sue, Jo, Matthew, Julie, Dee, Howard, Scott, Jacqui, Alan & Kevin.

# CONTENTS

# ACKNOWLEDGEMENTS

Writing *Martha and the Maids of the Square Table* has been, in many ways, a homecoming for me.

This book is a tribute to the many people who have walked alongside me throughout my career in Learning and Development, those who taught me, challenged me, trusted me, and grew with me. Also, to the thousands of leaders, managers, and learners across the world who sat with me in classrooms, questioned alongside me, reflected with me, and sometimes laughed with me as new understanding took shape: this book is for you.

Thank you for every conversation.

Thank you for every question.

Thank you for every challenge you brought into the room.

Thank you for every story you trusted me with.

Thank you for every moment when you allowed me to guide you, and for every moment when you taught me something in return.

Many of you will recognise echoes of familiar exercises, metaphors, moments, and lessons within these pages. If you see yourself in Martha, or in the wonderfully chaotic cast around her, that is intentional. Leadership is not neat or linear. It is human, emotional, complex, and deeply personal, and it is shaped by all of us who show up, imperfectly, and try again.

# PROLOGUE

## The Missing Banquet

The year was around AD 600, when men were warriors, battles were bloody, and employee induction programmes had... well, room for improvement.

The dawn sun crawled over the battlefield of Llongborth, illuminating the aftermath of a surprisingly swift victory.

King Arthur, resplendent in armour dented only where it made him look more heroic, surveyed the smouldering field with great satisfaction. "Well done, my knights; victory is once again ours," he proclaimed.

Sir Lancelot, who never missed an opportunity to praise the King (or himself), stepped forward. "Without you, my King, we would not have won this bloody battle."

Arthur shook his head with modest theatricality. "I cannot win a battle alone; I need you all. Together, we have won this day."

Sir Galahad, earnest as ever, nodded. "A formidable team, my lord."

"That we are," Arthur agreed. "And therefore unbeatable. But for now…" He paused dramatically as his stomach rumbled loud enough to startle a nearby crow. "We grow tired and hungry. Let us return to Camelot. A victorious meal awaits us." He turned to one of his young pages, a wiry boy named Horace, whose helmet was at least three sizes too large. "Boy! Run ahead and inform the head cook at the castle of our return. Tell them we need a banquet fit for royalty at 2.00pm this afternoon."

"Yes, my lord!" Horace squeaked, turning on his heel and sprinting towards Camelot with all the enthusiasm, and none of the job satisfaction, of a medieval intern.

The knights gathered their equipment and trudged homeward, eager for stew, bread, and the chance to boast exaggerated tales of personal heroism. They did not know, of course, that the true battle was waiting for them in the castle kitchens.

*****

By noon, the horns of Camelot blared triumphantly as Arthur and his knights rode through the gates. Guinevere hurried out to greet them, her gown billowing dramatically, as though she had been practising her entrance for just such an occasion.

"My darling Arthur, I was so worried about you!"

Arthur chuckled affectionately. "What have I told you, Guinevere? With the loyalty of the best knights in the world, you need not worry."

Lancelot, always eager to be included in Arthur's relational metaphors, chimed in, "Come, my lord, let us gather at the Round Table and feast our glorious victory."

Guinevere raised a delicate eyebrow. "Are you... expecting to eat this afternoon my dear?"

Arthur blinked. "Do we not feast after every victory?"

"Yes," she said carefully, "but if you recall, before you left, our Head Chef met an untimely... departure from this world."

Arthur winced as a vivid image popped into his mind. The former Head Chef, in a pristine kitchen, choking dramatically on an apple while a perfectly organised banquet lay untouched beside him. It had been a great tragedy, but an oddly tidy one.

"Yes, indeed. Poor chap. Did the agency not send a replacement, as I asked?"

"They did," Guinevere replied, "but... let us just say standards have slipped these last few months since Martha joined us."

Arthur's mind conjured a new image. The same kitchen, but now filthy, littered, and grimier than a stable floor, where a woman called Martha sat smoking and flicking ash into a bubbling pot of stew as though it was seasoning. It horrified him.

3

"Can she not cook?" Arthur asked, already afraid of the answer.

"She… cannot," Guinevere confirmed, "and her cleanliness leaves a lot to be desired."

"Well," Arthur sighed, "let us see what Martha and her maids can produce for us this fine afternoon. I sent Horace ahead to inform her of our arrival, so all will be fine, I am sure."

They all headed inside, blissfully unaware of the culinary carnage awaiting them. The knights gathered at the great Round Table, empty plates before them, empty goblets in hand, and empty stomachs echoing around the hall.

Arthur drummed his fingers on the polished wood. "It will be here soon," he said confidently. "We are simply a little early."

"Three days early," Lancelot corrected, stretching smugly. "I never thought they would surrender so quickly."

Arthur raised his empty goblet. "A fine victory, one we cannot even toast."

A long silence followed. An exceptionally long silence. In fact, a very extraordinarily long silence.

"And what exactly is the hold-up?" Bedivere whispered. "Do you think we can help, perhaps?"

Arthur cleared his throat. "Has anyone ever been to the kitchens?"

A chorus of "No, my lord!" erupted.

Not a single knight had ever ventured into the subterranean culinary labyrinth.

"It cannot be that hard to find," Arthur reasoned.

Geraint offered, "I believe it is below us, my lord."

Lancelot with a flick of his hair said, "I believe it is to the left of the grand staircase."

Bedivere scoffed. "No, that's the library."

Arthur frowned. "The library is on the second floor?"

Lancelot countered, "No, Guinevere's bedroom is on the second floor."

Arthur froze.

The room froze. Several knights stopped mid-breath.

"And how," Arthur asked dangerously softly, "would you know that?"

Lancelot gulped. "I was... looking for the kitchen. One night. When hungry."

Arthur narrowed his eyes. "And you believe the kitchen would be on the second floor?"

"Well... no."

"So?" asked Arthur in a low, stern voice.

Lancelot sighed. "So… the kitchen is not on the second floor. Nor is it to the left of the staircase. Which means it must be below us."

Geraint raised a hand. "I just said that."

Arthur ignored him. "Well then, how does one get down there?"

"The staircase in the corner," Geraint said. "It leads directly to the kitchens. If you recall, that is where the maids enter from when serving."

Arthur stood. "I imagine this staircase leads down to the kitchens, as this is where the maids come up from when they serve."

Geraint's eyes widened. "Again, I just said that."

Arthur turned dramatically to his knights. "Let us not forget Sir Geraint. A brave knight whose sacrifice in the Battle of Llongborth shall never be forgotten."

Geraint sputtered. "What do you mean sacrifice? I am not…" He began to fade. His voice wobbled. "I am right heeere…" Then, poof. He vanished entirely.

Arthur placed a solemn hand on his heart. "Standing here, I can almost feel that he was nearby. His spirit lives on in all of us."

Arthur raised his hands. "My knights, let us take a moment to honour Geraint. Brave warrior. Loyal companion. But terrible at accepting when the King has spoken."

The knights bowed their heads.

Lancelot added, "He had a wonderful horse."

Gawain sniffed. "A loyal steed."

Bedivere muttered, "Can I have it?"

Arthur glared. "Not now, Bedivere." He continued, "Geraint fell bravely in the heat of battle, despite the fact that no one remembers seeing him fall."

A hush fell. A dramatic hush. The kind of hush that would later confuse historians.

"Let us observe a moment of silence," Arthur concluded.

They did. A long one. Much longer than Geraint deserved.

Then Arthur, reinvigorated, marched towards the hidden staircase. The stairwell was dark, cobwebbed, and smelled faintly of forgotten soups. Arthur lit a torch, coughing as dust billowed like ancient confetti. "My, it is dark down here," he remarked, waving away cobwebs. "Looks as though no one has used this stairwell since we left."

At the bottom, he reached a heavy wooden door, locked, bolted, and at war with the concept of entry. Arthur knocked. Nothing. Arthur pounded. Still nothing. He hammered with royal fury. Inside, some voices stirred. Martha sat in a worn chair by the fire, a cigarette dangling from her lips, ash flicking lazily into a pot of something bubbling unhappily. Maids and cooks lounged around a table, filing nails, reading questionable magazines, and radiating the energy of employees who had mastered the art of appearing busy.

THUD. THUD. THUD.

"Who the blazes is that?" Martha snapped. "Do they not know we clock off at 2.00pm?!"

More banging.

Martha shouted, "There's no one here!"

"Yes, there is," came Arthur's voice.

"How do you know that?" Martha challenged.

"I can hear you in there," Arthur shouted back.

Martha squeaked loudly, "We are rats! Very hungry rats!"

The maids snorted with laughter.

Arthur sighed. "This is King Arthur. Open the door."

"And I," Martha retorted, "am Queen Martha. And I say it stays shut!"

Arthur pinched the bridge of his nose in despair. "Are you defying my orders?"

"Arthur does not return for another three days. So, you cannot be him," she called back smugly.

"The battle finished early!"

"Battles do not finish early!"

"This one did!"

"Well, we finish at 2.00pm, when the King's not here!"

Arthur, finally losing patience, roared, "Open this door immediately!"

Martha relented. "Cissy, open the door and let the man in."

Cissy, as downtrodden as any medieval intern, rose, complaining loudly about why she always had to do everything. She turned the large key and tugged at the bolt, which did not budge. Martha stomped over, shoved Cissy aside, and opened the door with one mighty yank.

Arthur stepped inside, jaw slack as he surveyed the chaos. "You must be Martha," he said slowly.

"That would be me, alright. And you must be the court jester."

Cissy whispered, "King Arthur…"

The maids curtsied.

Martha scoffed. "Do not be silly. This is not King Arthur; he is far too young and good-looking."

"You're fired!" Arthur declared.

And so began… negotiations.

Martha pleaded dramatically. She appealed for fairness. She mentioned her six children. She insisted she had never had training. She claimed she did not know the job. She declared she had never been taught leadership. And she hinted heavily that future employment tribunals might not look kindly on his decision.

Arthur, always the reasonable king (except during sword-related outbursts), relented. He would give her personal training to improve her performance in the kitchen and across Camelot, learning the art of leadership and management. She would have ten weeks to fix everything. Beginning tomorrow.

"But first," he said, "a fine banquet will be placed on the Round Table upstairs, just as I had instructed Horace to tell you."

"But no Horace came here to see me, my lord, and tell me that," she said, shaking her head.

At that point, Horace appeared from behind the scullery door and re-created the scene from earlier in the day, with the help of Cissy playing Martha.

"Are you the new head cook?" he asked hopefully.

"Maybe I am, maybe I am not," Cissy replied, feigning Martha's voice.

"Who is, then?"

"Who's asking?"

"Horace. King Arthur has sent me," he said with a broad, cheeky smile.

Cissy scoffed, as Martha had. "Been on the battlefield with Arthur, have you? Do not make me laugh."

"I have! And he returns this afternoon at 2.00pm and wants a huge banquet, fit for a king!"

"Run along. Arthur's not back for three days. You just want a free meal."

"But…"

"GO!"

Horace went to leave once again, but before he left, he and Cissy took a bow to the applause being given by the other maids and cooks in the room.

Martha shrugged. "Well… you did not expect me to believe him, did you?"

King Arthur turned on his heel and headed towards the door. "You have one hour to have a meal ready for us upstairs at the Round Table. I am guessing a full royal banquet is too much to ask for now, shall I call for pizza delivery myself?"

Martha replied, "I can do cheese and biscuits with French bread and pâté, but it's probably best you call for pizzas!"

King Arthur turned and looked long and hard at Martha. "Tomorrow, at 9.00am sharp, I expect you to be at my table, with pens and paper at the ready, ready to learn."

Martha took a long, hard drag on her cigarette and held his stare as long as she could before looking away and coughing out the smoke, she had tried to hold in. "Fine, I will be there," she said, realising this battle was one that she had lost.

# CHAPTER ONE

## The Day Martha Became a Leader
## (Against Her Better Judgement)
### Leadership & Motivation

The next morning at 8.55am, Martha shuffled into the Round Table chamber with bags, papers, and a cigarette hanging from her mouth like a weary chimney.

King Arthur immediately confiscated it and posted several "No Smoking" signs around the room.

Martha stared, aghast. "It'll never catch on," she said, blowing out the last of her smoke.

King Arthur just sighed. He lifted his sword, the ruby glowing as it projected an image onto the stone wall.

**LEADERSHIP & MOTIVATION**
**THE WAY OF THE FUTURE**
by King Arthur

King Arthur asked, "How would you define what a leader is?"

Martha replied, "That is simple, King Arthur. It is someone that makes sure everyone gets their heads down and does the job. And if not, you kick their behind. *Hard.*"

King Arthur groaned.

She sighed. "Got that one wrong, I guess, aye, King Arthur?"

King Arthur replied, "Please, Martha, just call me Arthur, as the author is getting tired of typing '*King*' all the time." He then clicked his ruby again as if it was a remote control.

# DEFINITION OF A LEADER

'Anyone who has the responsibility for the work of at least one other person and has the formal authority over them.'

Martha proudly declared she had four cooks, three maids, two helping hands, and a partridge in a pear tree.

Arthur looked to the floor and breathed in deeply. Looking up he asked Martha to write her own definition down. She moved to the flipchart in the corner of the room with great speed and wrote without thinking.

Then she rewrote her own definition on a flip chart in the corner of the room.

**MARTHA'S DEFINITION**
**'A classic case of multiple responsibilities, limited authority, and high accountability.'**

Arthur laughed, because she wasn't far wrong.

"Leadership can create issues when you are not always given the authority to get things done, but hold all the responsibility and are ultimately accountable for everything and everyone around you," he said with a grin.

Arthur once again clicked the ruby in the sword. It flickered, pulsed, and then flared into a bright magical projection against the castle wall.

ADAPTABLE, ANALYTICAL, APPRAISALS, BRIEFINGS, CHAIRING MEETINGS, COACHING, COMMUNICATING, CONTINUOUSLY IMPROVING, CREATING, CUSTOMER FOCUSED, DECISION MAKING, DELEGATING, DISCIPLINING, DRIVING, EMPOWERING, FEEDBACK, GOAL SETTING, HONESTY, IMPLEMENTING, INFLUENCING, INITIATIVE, INTEGRITY, INTERVIEWING SKILLS, JUDGEMENTAL, LISTENING, MANAGING CHANGE, MENTORING, MOTIVATING, NEGOTIATING, PERSONAL DEVELOPMENT, PRESENTATION SKILLS, PRIORITISING, PROBLEM SOLVING, PROCESS MANAGEMENT, PROJECT MANAGEMENT, QUALITY MANAGEMENT, QUESTIONING, RELIABLE, RESILIENT, RESPONSIBILITY, SENSITIVITY, STRESS MANAGEMENT, TEAMWORK, TIME MANAGEMENT, TRAINING & TRUST!

"With leadership comes many things, some are characteristics you will need, others are roles you will need to play, others are responsibilities you will have, and some are behaviours you will need to display," he said, as the words appeared around the walls of the room like a cloud burst.

He spoke them out loud, almost in a cinematic voice, then they faded as quickly as they appeared.

"Here is a vision one week from today. This vision is what *would* happen without this leadership training and your understanding of the role you play here as Leader of the Kitchen."

The projection shimmered, then formed into a moving scene…

The kitchen was somehow even worse than today. If 'mess' had a mess, and that mess had tripped over another mess, the result would be the scene before them. The air hung thick with smoke, steam, and resentment as the future projected vision unfolded. Martha was slumped in her favourite chair, the sagging one that creaked under her sense of authority more than her weight. A cigarette dangled precariously from her bottom lip, ash threatening to fall like volcanic debris. Her boots were on the table, dangerously close to a mixing bowl containing what might once have been batter, now resembling wet mortar, and her eyes were closed, drifting in and out of sleep. Around her, the team were gathered in a huddle, not working, not cooking, not even pretending to. Simply existing in a state of communal misery.

In the scene Cissy sighed dramatically, the sigh of a woman whose will to live had been slowly eroded by years of emotional erosion condensed into seven days.

Morag muttered, "I have just about had enough of this place."

"You and me both," Cissy replied, arms folded. "Yesterday she told me that if I did not 'buck my ideas up', I'd be fired."

Morag leaned in. "That's nothing. I made two lovely apple tarts for Lancelot. Perfect crust. Glossy glaze. Dusting of cinnamon. Martha took one look at them and ate both."

Cissy gasped. "Both?!"

"Aye," Morag said bitterly. "Then she told Lancelot I dropped them. And that we'd run out of apples. He was none too pleased; I can tell you."

Cissy shook her head. "She should be fired. She's a lazy, no-good, for-nothing old moo-cow." Her whisper echoed off the stone walls.

Martha's eyes snapped open. "I heard that," she growled. "Now get cooking and cleaning while I create visions in my head." She tapped her forehead twice for emphasis, causing ash to fall into the mortar bowl.

The girls exchanged glances. They did not move. Not out of defiance, but out of sheer hopelessness.

Seeing this, Martha pushed herself upright with the stiff, resentful energy of a woman rising from a throne she believed she deserved. "What's wrong with you all?" Martha barked. "We've got work to do! Come on, shift yourselves!"

No one moved. The room was as silent as a tomb. Except tombs are peaceful. This was the silence of suppressed rage and low morale.

Martha placed her hands on her hips. "Useless, the lot of you!"

Morag muttered under her breath, "She'd shout at sunshine for being too bright."

Cissy added, "She'd shout at bread for not toasting itself."

Morag nodded. "She'd shout at herself in the mirror, then argue back."

The maids giggled, but it was the sad kind of giggle, the kind that said, 'I am laughing because if I don't, I will scream and run away from here and never look back.'

Martha clapped her hands together. "Right! Team meeting!"

The maids groaned.

She strutted (in her own mind) to the centre of the kitchen, adopting what she imagined was a power stance, though to everyone else it looked like she was suffering the early onset of cramp or wind. "Listen up!" she announced. "I have decided we need more motivation around here."

Cissy perked up slightly. Maybe this was good?

Morag whispered, "Maybe she's changed…"

Martha continued, "So, I am introducing a new system. It is called… the Stick Method."

The maids' faces fell. Martha held up an actual stick. Not metaphorically. Not symbolically. An actual stick.

Cissy gasped. "Where did you even get that?!"

"Outside," Martha said proudly. "Training tool. Inspirational, it is. Now then, if you mess up, I give you a tap with the Stick of Improvement."

Morag blinked. "That'll hurt."

"Exactly!" Martha boomed.

Cissy raised a tentative hand. "Isn't there a… Carrot Method?"

Martha rolled her eyes so dramatically she nearly saw her own brain. "Don't be stupid, Cissy. Carrots are for soups and asses."

The maids exchanged the kind of look that said, 'We are one stick-tap away from forming a union.'

Cissy whispered, "I cannot work like this."

Morag whispered back, "Neither can I."

Martha marched over. "I heard that! Now get moving before I bring out a bigger stick!"

Cissy's eyes welled up.

Morag stood up. "You always treat us like dirt! You don't listen, you don't help, and you don't teach us anything!"

Martha scoffed. "Teaching? Motivating? Listening? That's not my job!"

The maids stared.

Morag said, "You're literally our boss."

Martha froze. Thought. Processed. Rejected the information. Lit another cigarette.

"Rubbish," she muttered. "If you don't motivate yourselves, I cannot help you."

Cissy whispered to Morag, "She doesn't even know what motivation means."

Morag sighed. "She thinks it is something you sprinkle on a pie."

The maids laughed weakly.

Martha glared. "Enough laughing! Get back to work! And I want the floor scrubbed until I can see my own reflection!"

Cissy whispered, "Imagine seeing that reflection."

Morag nodded. "That's punishment enough."

At this moment, the ceiling dripped slightly, not for symbolic effect, but because Martha had neglected to fix a leak for months.

Morag sat down heavily. "I cannot do it. I cannot scrub another floor. I cannot bake another tart. I cannot listen to her anymore."

Cissy shook her head. "Me neither."

The team collectively slumped. Their energy was gone. Their enthusiasm shrivelled. Their commitment evaporated like steam from an unattended cauldron.

Martha looked around at the unmoving staff and declared triumphantly, "Well! If you will not work... I will just sit here and wait until you do!" Which she did. Feet up. Arms crossed. Face smug. A complete triumph of managerial incompetence.

The future vision projection on the wall now faded away, and the ruby went dull.

Martha stared at the wall, horrified. Wide-eyed. Speechless. For the first time in her life. "Well," she muttered eventually, "that went downhill fast."

Arthur folded his arms. "Indeed. That, Martha, is what happens when you lead without motivation."

Martha sniffed. "They were very rude."

Arthur looked at her flatly. "You brought a stick into a team meeting."

"Well, I will not do that again," she said defensively.

"To motivate people," Arthur explained gently, "you must understand what makes them want to work. Not force them into it."

Martha nodded slowly. "So... no sticks?"

"No sticks," he said, clicking the ruby remote once again on his sword.

# WHAT IS MOTIVATION?

**'Motivation is the reason why you do something, or the drive that pushes you into action'**

*SIMPLIFIED*

**'Motivation is what makes you want to do something.'**

Arthur decided it was time to introduce Martha to intrinsic and extrinsic motivators. He clasped his hands behind his back, pacing thoughtfully as the last flickers of the motivation definition projection faded from the wall. "Martha," he said at last, "if you are to lead your team effectively, you must understand motivation."

Martha nodded confidently, the confident nod of someone who absolutely *did not* understand motivation but assumed it could not be too different from peeling potatoes.

Arthur continued, "Tell me, Martha... do you know the difference between intrinsic and extrinsic motivation?"

Martha grinned proudly. "Oh yes. Absolutely. Clear as day."

Arthur's eyebrows lifted. "You do?"

"Course I do," she said, folding her arms. "Intrinsic motivation is when you poke someone with something sharp on the inside, like in the ribs. And extrinsic motivation is when you do it on the outside, like on the backside with a stick."

Arthur stared at her.

Martha beamed, clearly delighted with her answer.

He inhaled slowly through his nose, in the way of a man who had once slain dragons but currently faced a far more dangerous foe, ignorance fuelled by confidence. "Martha," he said carefully, "no one is poking anyone. On the inside or the outside."

Martha frowned. "Then what's the point of the stick? I thought motivating meant... prod them until they get moving."

"NO!" Arthur blurted, louder than he intended.

Martha blinked, startled.

Arthur collected himself. "Let us... take a step back."

He gestured his sword and ruby dramatically, conjuring a glowing magical subtitle hovering in mid-air above him.

# INTRINSIC MOTIVATION

Arthur said, "Intrinsic motivation means doing something because you *enjoy it*, or find satisfaction in doing it well."

Martha tilted her head. "Enjoying work...?"

"Yes."

"On purpose?"

"Yes."

She squinted, looking deeply suspicious. "This is one of those future ideas, isn't it?"

Arthur chose to ignore that. "To put it simply," he said, "intrinsic motivation comes from within."

Martha perked up. "Ah! So intrinsic means inside!"

"Yes!" Arthur exclaimed, relieved.

"Like indigestion!"

"No!" he snapped. Then softened. "Similar prefix. Entirely different meaning."

Martha nodded slowly, though the vague expression on her face suggested the prefix was the only part she'd absorbed.

Arthur snapped his fingers again, producing the next shimmering subtitle.

## EXTRINSIC MOTIVATION

"This," Arthur said, "is motivation that comes from outside. Rewards. Encouragement. Praise. Tangible things."

Martha nodded vigorously. "Ah yes, outside things, like sticks."

"No! *Not sticks!*"

"Food?" she said quickly.

Arthur sighed. "*Yes…* food can be an extrinsic motivator, if used correctly."

Martha brightened. "Good! Because I have always said, a sausage roll speaks louder than words."

"A very crude summary," Arthur said, "but surprisingly accurate."

Martha continued, "We could have pizza Fridays, or Thirsty Thursdays, when everyone gets a smoothie of their choice!" she beamed.

Arthur pressed on. "I cannot see that catching on. It is a little bit basic, if you ask me. Extrinsic motivation is when someone works because they want the reward or wish to avoid punishment."

Martha gasped. "Like when my mother told me to scrub the floors, or she'd make me eat her cabbage soup!"

Arthur paused. "Disturbingly... yes. That is technically extrinsic motivation."

Martha shuddered. "Worst soup I ever had. Motivated me for years."

"I am sure it did," Arthur murmured.

Arthur clapped his hands together and the shimmering subtitles vanished before them. "So, Martha, perhaps you can summarise. What is intrinsic motivation?"

Martha puffed up proudly. "Intrinsic motivation is when you work hard because you like soup!"

Arthur blinked. "How... how did soup get into this again?"

"You said it comes from within," Martha insisted. "And soup sits within! Especially bad soup. Deep within, very, very deep within."

Arthur pinched the bridge of his nose once again in despair. "*No!* Intrinsic motivation is when you work hard because you want to, because you enjoy the task or feel fulfilled by it."

Martha frowned. "Sounds very suspicious."

"And extrinsic motivation?" Arthur asked carefully.

Martha declared confidently, "That one's easy. It is when you work hard because someone's waving a sausage roll at you."

Arthur threw his hands in the air. "Close enough."

He waved his sword, and glowing words arranged themselves into a perfectly clear set of examples in the air around them.

# INTRINSIC MOTIVATION
## Comes from within

**Wanting to learn a new skill
Feeling proud of good work
Finding joy in the task
Being curious and being praised
Helping others
Sense of achievement**

# EXTRINSIC MOTIVATION
## Comes from outside

**Rewards, time off, days out, learning events
Food and treats
Financial recognition
Avoiding punishment
Winning competitions**

Arthur tapped the words gently. "Martha, to lead effectively, you must find out what motivates each person, intrinsic or extrinsic."

She stared thoughtfully at the words. "Well…" she said, "Cissy and Morag definitely work for extrinsic motivation."

Arthur raised an eyebrow. "How so?"

Martha smirked. "They'd do anything for a slice of my cherry pie."

Arthur sighed. "Then let us put that to good use."

Arthur guided Martha through a heartfelt apology to Cissy and Morag. She offered teamwork… and cherry pie as an extrinsic motivator for when the kitchen is sparkling clean. The maids agreed on the promise of the cherry pie. Together the three of them, with some occasional help from Arthur, cleaned the kitchen.

Four hours later, Martha basked in the sparkling surroundings. "This feels… lovely," she admitted.

Arthur nodded. "That's a sense of achievement, an intrinsic motivator. And the tea and pie are extrinsic."

Arthur raised his sword once again, and Martha sighed loudly, the ruby now glowing like an overworked magical slide projector.

"Martha," he said, "there is another way to understand motivation. One that will help you better lead your team."

Martha wrinkled her nose. "Another way? How many ways are there?"

"Thousands," Arthur replied. "But this one comes from a wise scholar who will be born many centuries from now, a man named **David McClelland**."

Martha blinked. "That's a funny name."

Arthur ignored that. "His theory," he continued, "explains that people are motivated by three main *needs*, things they crave, things they seek, or things they naturally gravitate towards."

Martha scratched her head. "Like cherry pie?"

"No," Arthur said firmly, though privately he acknowledged pie could easily be a fourth category. He waved the sword again. Three glowing words appeared on the wall.

## ACHIEVEMENT - POWER - AFFILIATION

Martha gasped. "Oh, we're learning spellings now!"

"No! These are motivational needs."

"Oh. Right. Shame."

Arthur pointed his sword at the first glowing word.

## ACHIEVEMENT

"Achievement," he said with great gusto, "the desire to

accomplish great things. Knights who possess this, need to seek challenges, goals, puzzles, quests, anything that proves their worth."

The projection shifted to a vision of Lionel and Percival.

They were kneeling dramatically beside the Holy Grail, polishing it, measuring it, writing reports on it, performing risk assessments on it, arguing over whether it should be clockwise or counterclockwise on the ceremonial plinth.

Martha squinted. "What are they doing?"

Arthur sighed proudly. "Achievers. They adore goals."

Martha watched the two knights fuss over the Grail like doting parents over a newborn.

She nodded. "So, they're like the people who love making lists."

Arthur tilted his head. "Exactly."

"Lists for everything," Martha continued. "Lists for cleaning. Lists for recipes. Lists for things they need to remember because their memory is shocking."

"Yes," Arthur said slowly, "achievers enjoy structure and purpose."

"And then more lists about the lists!"

Arthur pinched his nose. "Yes. Fine. That too."

The projection showed Percival carrying a massive scroll titled:

**HOLY GRAIL**

Project Plan

A 47 Step Implementation Strategy

Martha whistled. "That's more steps than my washing routine."

"Achievers chase excellence," Arthur explained. "They want to hit targets, reach goals, complete quests."

Martha grinned. "So basically, they're show-offs."

Arthur opened his mouth to object, then closed it. "Moving on," he said diplomatically.

## POWER

The glowing word POWER expanded dramatically, accompanied by a thunderous sound effect. Arthur definitely hadn't programmed it that way, but pretended he had.

The wall now showed Gawain standing triumphantly on a hill, sword raised, cloak blowing majestically behind him, barking instructions on the importance of breathing properly in battle. Except... he wasn't on a hill. He was standing on the stump of a tree and insisting it was a hill.

Martha frowned. "Why is he on a tree?"

Arthur gave a long-suffering sigh. "Gawain has a high need for power. He enjoys influence. Status. Control. Being listened to. Leading others."

Martha watched Gawain barking his orders at a bewildered squire who was idly standing around. "Is he teaching that man how to breathe in battle?" she asked.

"Yes," Arthur replied. "He believes inhaling should be done with more vigour in battle."

Martha snorted. "He sounds exhausting."

"Power-motivated individuals," Arthur explained, "often want authority. They want to be the best. They want to shape the world around them."

Martha thought about this, eyes narrowing thoughtfully.

"So, what you're saying is... Gawain likes being the big bossy boots."

Arthur paused. "Yes, Martha. That is... one way of putting it."

Gawain struck a pose on the stump that was somehow even more dramatic than the first.

Martha squinted. "He's not wearing trousers."

Arthur groaned and quickly waved his sword to move to the next scene.

## AFFILIATION

The final word, AFFILIATION, glowed pink for some reason. The projection shifted to Lancelot, surrounded by at least six admiring ladies, all leaning in, giggling, fluttering lashes, and generally looking ready to faint at his mere presence.

Arthur stared. "I specifically told him not to flirt during training hours."

Martha gasped. "Look at him! He's got more women than I have got spoons!"

Lancelot winked back out of the projection to Martha, as if aware of the different dimensions.

Arthur cleared his throat. "Affiliation is the need to be liked, Martha. To belong. To build relationships. To be accepted."

"So, he's needy," Martha said bluntly.

Arthur bristled. "He is warm. And friendly. And supportive."

"He's needy," Martha repeated.

"And he enjoys companionship."

"He's very needy."

Arthur closed his eyes. "Fine. Yes. He has… a considerable need for affiliation and affection."

Martha leaned in closer. "So, he wants everyone to like him, does he?"

"Precisely."

She snorted. "Even the horses like him."

"He does spend a lot of time in the stables," Arthur said, then quickly added, "helping with chores! And being… personable."

Martha folded her arms. "He knows where Guinevere's bedroom is."

Arthur stiffened. "We do not need to talk about that." Arthur turned to her expectantly. "Now, Martha. Can you summarise the three needs?"

Martha nodded eagerly. "Well… achievement is when you're a list-obsessed show-off who wants to win trophies."

Arthur grimaced. "That is… not *entirely* wrong."

"And power is when you want to be the bossy-boots-in-chief."

Arthur winced. "Close enough."

"And affiliation is when you're so needy you cannot walk into a room without making ten new friends and possibly kissing half of them."

Arthur closed his eyes. "Dear heavens."

Martha threw up her hands. "But I understand it! I do! Everyone wants different things, so you need to treat each person differently to motivate them!"

Arthur snapped his eyes open. His jaw dropped. "That is… exactly correct."

Martha beamed.

Arthur beamed.

Then Martha added proudly, "So Gawain gets a crown, Lionel gets homework, and Lancelot gets… well… whatever Guinevere gives him."

Arthur choked. "No! Martha! That is not…" He tapped the ruby once more for the next magical projection.

## MCCLELLAND'S
### THREE MOTIVATIONAL NEEDS

### ACHIEVEMENT

*People who want to excel*
Love goals and challenges
Seek improvement
Prefer tasks they can master

### POWER

*People who want influence*
Enjoy being in charge
Thrive on responsibility
Seek authority and leadership

### AFFILIATION

*People who seek connection*
Want to feel liked and included
Prefer teamwork
Thrive in warm, social environments

Arthur lowered his sword. "That, Martha, is what drives my knights. And it is what will drive your team, once you understand them."

Martha thought deeply for a moment. "So, what you're saying is… leadership isn't one-size-fits-all?"

Arthur smiled. "Exactly."

Martha sniffed. "Seems like a lot of work."

Arthur nodded. "It is."

She brightened. "Good job I am clever, then."

Arthur blinked. "Yes. Good... job."

Finally, Arthur decided it might be a good thing to offer Martha some guidance on motivating herself. He lifted the sword again, its ruby glowing with an almost sympathetic warmth. "Martha," he said gently, "before we finish today's lesson, there is one final thing you must understand."

Martha folded her arms. "If it is about carrots and sticks again, I have returned the stick to nature."

"No," Arthur said patiently. "*This is about you.*"

Martha blinked. "Me?"

"Yes. You must learn how to motivate... yourself."

Martha's eyes narrowed. "I don't like where this is going."

Arthur sighed, raised the sword, and clicked the ruby remote. The ruby flashed. The wall shimmered. And then a title appeared:

## MARTHA AT HER LOWEST POINT

The projection showed Martha one week prior. Slumped in her filthy chair. Hair askew. Boots on the table. Smoke drifting lazily from a half-smoked cigarette that wasn't even lit properly. Her apron stained with something unidentifiable (possibly soup, possibly a crime). Her expression a mixture of boredom, despair, and mild gastric discomfort. She stared at the ceiling, muttering to herself, "What's the point...? The floor's dirty. The staff hate me. The stew hates me. Even the cockroaches around here have higher standards."

Present-day Martha clasped a hand to her chest. "I look awful!"

Arthur raised an eyebrow. "This was... last Tuesday when we returned from battle."

Martha gasped. "Tuesday?! I thought that was... at least five years ago!"

"No. Tuesday."

The projection of Martha groaned loudly enough to shake imaginary dust off the rafters. "I cannot do this. I am not cleaning anything. No one appreciates me. There's no point trying. I will just sit here and slowly fossilise." She slumped further down the chair, limbs dangling like a depressed scarecrow.

Present Martha winced. "Oh, dear heavens, I look like a sad sack of potatoes."

Arthur nodded sympathetically. "This, Martha, is what demotivation looks like."

Projection Martha let out a theatrical sigh and muttered, "Everything hurts. Especially my ambition."

Present Martha pointed. "Lies! I have never had ambition."

Arthur gave her a pointed look.

She whispered, "Alright… maybe a tiny bit, once upon a time."

As projection Martha continued wallowing, present Martha leaned closer to the image, squinting hard.

Projection Martha muttered, "Maybe if I close my eyes very tight, all my problems will disappear."

"NO, THEY WILL NOT!" present Martha barked back at herself.

Arthur blinked. "Martha?"

She jabbed a finger at the projection. "Listen here, you lazy old moo-cow! Sitting around feeling sorry for yourself isn't going to fix your mess!"

Projection Martha took a drag of her half-dead cigarette and grumbled, "It is all hopeless…"

"NO IT ISN'T!" present Martha shouted, stepping closer. "Look at you! Feeling sorry for yourself will not clean a kitchen or motivate the team!"

Arthur hid a smile behind his hand. This was working brilliantly.

Projection Martha sighed dramatically again and whimpered, "I should just stay here. Forever."

Present Martha threw her hands up. "OH, STOP BEING SO DRAMATIC! GET UP! WASH YOUR

FACE! SCRUB THE FLOOR! MAKE A CUP OF TEA! DO SOMETHING!"

Projection Martha blinked slowly, as if considering it.

Present Martha shouted louder. **"DON'T 'CONSIDER' IT!** *J.F.D.I.!*"

Arthur nodded. "Excellent, Martha. Tell her what she needs to do."

Present Martha planted her fists on her hips, full drill-sergeant mode. "RIGHT THEN!" Martha shouted rather aggressively at the projection. "Here's what you need to do, and you're going to blooming well do it!" She pointed dramatically and began pacing like a furious goose. "ONE: GET UP OUT OF THAT CHAIR!"

Projection Martha slowly straightened up.

"FASTER!" real Martha yelled. "You look like a sack of damp laundry!"

Projection Martha obeyed and got out of the chair.

"TWO: CLEAN THAT KITCHEN!"

Projection Martha looked around gloomily.

"DON'T PULL THAT FACE!" real Martha barked. "YOU MADE THAT MESS!"

Arthur muttered, "Well... technically the cooks and maids did..."

"NOT NOW, ARTHUR!"

Arthur promptly shut his mouth.

"THREE: STOP COMPLAINING AND START DOING!"

Projection Martha shuffled towards a broom.

"YES! PICK IT UP!" real Martha shouted. "Sweep the floor. Wipe that counter! Scrub those pans! Pretend you're filming a cleaning product advert!"

Projection Martha began half-heartedly sweeping and wiping things, smiling at the thought of being on television in an advert, if televisions existed, of course.

"FOUR: HAVE A CUP OF TEA IF YOU MUST, BUT NOT UNTIL YOU'VE EARNED IT!"

Projection Martha's eyes widened with terror.

"YES!" real Martha shouted triumphantly. "Fear the tea! Let it drive you forward!"

Arthur clicked the remote again and the projection gently faded. He turned to Martha with a kind smile. "*That*," he said, "is how you motivate yourself. A little self-compassion... a little self-direction... and occasionally shouting at yourself when you begin to spiral."

Martha was flushed but proud. "Well... she needed telling."

Arthur nodded. "Self-motivation is about knowing what lifts you, what pushes you forward, and what pulls you out of your darkest moments, like a cup of tea as a reward."

He raised the sword once more, and the final slide appeared:

# MOTIVATING YOURSELF

**Set clear goals**
**Become adaptable and resilient**
**Gain new knowledge and skills**
**Create a positive environment**
**Take initiative**
**Inspire others**
**Find fulfilment in everything you do**
**Reward yourself as others may not**

Martha nodded, softer now. "So... I cannot help others... unless I help myself first?"

Arthur smiled. "Exactly."

Martha sniffed. "Well, I suppose I'd better get working on me then."

Arthur chuckled. "I think you already have."

Martha straightened proudly. "And next time I see her," she pointed to where the projection had been, "I will make sure she behaves."

Arthur laughed. "That's the spirit, and so ends our first lesson," he said, as the ruby projections faded away.

Martha nodded, changed, only just a little, but enough to be on the right path.

Leadership had begun. Motivation had begun.

And the real comedy… was still yet to come.

# CHAPTER TWO

## Say What You Mean, Not What You Said
### Communication & Miscommunication

The morning sun rose over Camelot with the bright, unforgiving glare of a spotlight, the sort that exposes every flaw, every dust mote, and every curtain you absolutely meant to wash but never quite got around to. It streamed through the castle windows, landing squarely on the Round Table, where King Arthur sat, sipping tea and rehearsing patience like a monk preparing for a month-long vow of silence.

Today was Week Two of Martha's leadership training.

Arthur was ready.

Camelot was... cautiously optimistic.

The kitchen staff were terrified.

And Martha, somewhere below, in the depths of the castle, was currently wrestling with a mop that she insisted had 'an attitude problem'.

Arthur checked the time, albeit clocks had not been invented yet. But he had a reliable internal sense of 'Martha Time', which was always approximately seventeen minutes late, regardless of the situation.

Sure enough… a clatter erupted from the hallway. A pot rolled dramatically across the stone floor. A broom snapped in half. Someone swore. Loudly. And Martha burst into the Grand Hall like a woman pursued by a dragon, or at the very least, a very angry goose. Her hair was slightly singed. Her apron was on backwards. Her expression was one of furious triumph. "Morning, Arthur!" she announced proudly, as though she had not just created a noise reminiscent of a minor earthquake.

Arthur set his tea down delicately. "Good morning, Martha. Are you prepared for today's lesson?"

She slammed a stack of papers onto the table. "I am! I wrote down everything I remembered from last time."

Arthur glanced at the pages. They were blank. "Martha," he said gently, "these are empty."

She beamed. "Yes! Last week you taught me I cannot read or write properly yet, remember? So, I decided not to waste good paper. Saves the environment."

Arthur blinked twice. "Well… I suppose that is one way to look at it."

Martha nodded vigorously. "So, what are we learning today? More poking? More pie bribery? More shouting at myself?"

Arthur took a deep breath. "No, Martha. Today we are learning communication."

Martha frowned. "I talk all the time."

"Yes," Arthur said carefully. "That is, in fact... the problem." Arthur rose dramatically, pacing across the room with the gravitas of someone about to deliver a TED Talk fourteen hundred years early. "Martha," he began, "communication is the foundation of leadership. Without it, messages get lost, tasks go wrong, battles are missed, banquets go uneaten."

"...and knights end up in the wrong village?" Martha interrupted.

Arthur paused. "Yes. Exactly. How did you know?"

Martha scratched her chin. "Well... funny story. I sent Gawain and Bedivere to fetch eggs yesterday. Told them the hen farmer lived at the edge of Camelot. Turns out 'edge' sounds a lot like 'hedge'."

Arthur winced. "Oh no."

"Oh yes," Martha said. "They spent three hours interrogating shrubbery."

Arthur sighed. "And did they bring back any eggs?"

"Only one," Martha said, pulling a crushed object from her apron. "And now it is gone."

Arthur pressed a hand to his forehead. "Martha... communication is vital. If we cannot understand one another, we cannot lead. Which is why today's lesson begins with a scholar from the future."

Martha perked up. "Oh! Another wizard from the times ahead?"

"Not exactly," Arthur said, lifting Excalibur. "A great expert on communication, **Albert Mehrabian**."

The ruby flared. On the wall appeared glowing words:

# THE MEHRABIAN PRINCIPLE

### 7% Words
### 38% Tone of Voice
### 55% Body Language

Martha stared at the numbers. Then she burst out laughing. "Arthur, that makes no sense at all! If someone wants to tell me something, they tell me something! Words are words!"

Arthur shook his head. "No, Martha. Only 7% of communication is the words themselves. People judge your message mostly by how you say it, your tone and what your body does while you say it."

Martha squinted suspiciously. "So, if I tell someone they're doing a good job, but I am shouting, and waving a spoon at them... they will not believe me?"

Arthur nodded. "Correct."

"And if I say, 'you're useless' but I do it with a smile and a cuddle...?"

Arthur blinked. "No. No, Martha! They will still believe you think they are useless."

She shrugged. "Worth a try."

Arthur sighed. "Let us move to the next important concept, how messages travel." He clicked again.

## SHANNON–WEAVER MODEL

Sender → Message → Channel → Receiver → Feedback → Noise

Martha tilted her head. "Arthur... that's not communication. That's the recipe for my best soup."

Arthur exhaled slowly. "No. This is how communication works."

Martha stared harder. "Are you sure? Looks like soup."

Arthur pinched the bridge of his nose again, a gesture becoming dangerously habitual. "Martha, let me explain."

He pointed to each component. "**Sender** - the person sending the message."

"Me!" Martha said proudly.

"**Message** - the information being sent."

"Right. Like 'stop smoking'."

"Yes," said Arthur, "or 'please clean the kitchen,' or 'Arthur returns at 2.00pm'."

Martha's face fell. "Oh. That one."

"**Channel**," Arthur continued, "how the message is sent. Spoken words, writing, messenger boy called Horace."

"Or shouting at people from the top of the stairs," Martha added.

"I… suppose so."

"**Receiver** - the person getting the message."

"Usually someone terribly confused," Martha said.

Arthur ignored that. "**Feedback** - how they respond. This shows whether they understood."

Martha nodded. "Ah. So, when my maids look blankly at me for several seconds and then walk away… that's feedback?"

"Yes!" Arthur said, delighted. "Feedback showing, they did not understand."

Martha frowned. "I thought it meant they were rude."

"Sometimes it is both," Arthur admitted. "And the last one: **Noise**," he continued. "Noise is anything that distracts from the message."

Martha gasped. "Oh! Like Cissy crying, Morag banging pots, the stew bubbling, the rats squeaking, the roof leaking, the smoke filling the room."

"Yes!" Arthur interrupted. "All of that is noise!"

Martha nodded seriously. "So, what you're saying is… my entire kitchen… is noise."

Arthur paused. "Correct."

Martha shrugged. "Right. Explains a lot, does that soup."

Arthur stood tall. "Now, Martha, let us examine how you currently communicate."

Martha brightened. "Right-o!"

He cleared his throat. "Martha, please explain how you would tell a maid to bring more bread to the Round Table."

Martha threw her hands in the air, puffed out her chest, and shouted, "CISSY! BREAD! NOW!"

The sound echoed dramatically around the chamber. Arthur stared at her in horror. "Martha… that was not a request. That was a declaration of war."

"But it works," she insisted.

"No," Arthur said. "It achieves compliance. Not communication."

Martha folded her arms. "What's the difference?"

Arthur inhaled deeply. "Compliance is doing something because you were told. Communication is doing something because you understand."

Martha blinked slowly. "I thought those were the same thing."

"No," Arthur said. "And let me demonstrate." He raised his voice. "Lancelot!"

Lancelot poked his head around the door instantly. "Yes, my lord?"

"Could you please fetch us some bread?"

"Certainly, my lord!" Lancelot beamed and vanished.

Martha scoffed. "Oh, well that doesn't count. He likes you. He's highly affiliation motivated."

Arthur frowned. "Fine. Let us test with someone more neutral." He stood straight, took a calming breath, and called out, "Tristan! Would you kindly bring us some fresh bread?"

Tristan entered almost immediately. "My lord, I have already anticipated your need." He placed a platter of warm bread on the table, bowed, and exited.

Martha stared.

Arthur smiled. "Clear message. Respectful tone. Effective result."

Martha huffed. "Well, I could do that."

Arthur lifted his eyebrows. "Try."

Martha stood tall, puffed up, face determined. "Percival! If you're not too busy strutting about like a peacock, bring us some bread!"

Arthur winced.

Moments later, Percival returned. Not with bread. But with a sword drawn. "Who challenges my dignity?!" he roared.

Arthur immediately raised a hand. "Stand down, Percival. It was merely... a demonstration."

Percival sheathed the sword reluctantly. "Very well, my lord. But someone owes me an apology." He glared at Martha.

Martha smiled sweetly. "Sorry, Percival. I did not mean to ruffle your feathers."

He grunted and left.

Arthur sighed. "Martha... today might be a long day."

Arthur walked her through the Round Table Hall. "Martha, communication is not about shouting louder. It is about clarity." He gestured to the windows. "Noise is not just sound. It is anything that gets in the way of your message."

At that moment, a knight ran past, shouting, "THE SHEEP ARE IN THE ARMOURY AGAIN!"

Arthur pointed. "That. That is noise."

Martha nodded.

A maid rushed after him. "AND THE ARMOUR IS IN THE MOAT!"

Martha blinked. "Well… that explains the clanking."

Arthur exhaled. "Yes. More noise." Arthur gathered a group of knights and maids. "Martha, we will now play a game to show how messages get distorted."

Martha grinned. "Oh, I love games! Does it involve hitting people with things?"

"No," Arthur said firmly. "It is a listening game."

Martha's face fell. "Boring."

Arthur whispered into Bedivere's ear: "Arthur returns at dawn with fifteen horses."

Bedivere nodded solemnly, turned to the next knight, and whispered, "Arthur returns at lawn with fifty sausages."

That knight whispered, "Arthur returns with long sausages."

Next: "Arthur wants long sausages."

Then: "Arthur demands long sausages."

Then: "Arthur is angry about sausage length!"

Until the final message reached Cissy. "Martha! The King wants you to sort out his sausage before he explodes!"

Martha turned to Arthur indignantly. "Arthur, that is *not* appropriate behaviour for royalty. Let's hope Human Resources did not hear that."

Arthur massaged his temples. "That is precisely the point, Martha."

She leaned in thoughtfully. "So, what you're saying is… people are idiots."

Arthur groaned. "No, Martha. People mishear. Misunderstand. Assume. Forget. Add. Delete. Confuse."

Martha shrugged. "Same thing."

Arthur sighed. "Let us move on."

Arthur guided Martha back to the Round Table with the air of a teacher who knew the worst was behind them, but suspected the worst had also just begun. "Martha," he said gently, "communication is more than sending messages. It is also about how you *receive* them."

Martha nodded firmly. "That's easy. I receive messages all the time. I just don't reply."

Arthur blinked. "That… is exactly the problem."

She shrugged. "Replies take ages."

A long silence followed. Arthur breathed through it. "Martha," Arthur began, "today we must also practise written communication. You will write a simple note to one of your maids. A short instruction. Clear. Concise."

Martha puffed up proudly. "I can do that! Writing is easy! I just… improvise letters until they look right."

Arthur did not like the sound of that. She strutted to the table, snatched a quill, dipped it in ink with the enthusiasm of a woodpecker attacking a tree, and began scribbling furiously. Arthur leaned in. "Martha… what exactly are you writing?"

"A note! To Morag! Telling her to tidy up the pantry."

Arthur examined the page. It looked like a spider having a seizure. "Martha… that does not resemble any known language."

"It does!" she insisted. "It is written in my own handwriting!"

"That," Arthur said patiently, "is the problem."

She lifted the parchment proudly. "There! Clear instructions!"

Arthur squinted.

The note read: 'Mroag tidi panty or els.'

Martha nodded. "See? Straightforward."

Arthur rubbed his forehead. "Martha… that message could be interpreted in many unfortunate ways."

Just then, Morag walked in, saw the note, gasped, blushed crimson, fumed, and fainted. Arthur moved quickly and called on Lancelot to take Morag off for a fine cup of tea.

"Right," Arthur said. "Let's forget writing for now and move on to discuss non-verbal communication."

Martha crossed her arms. "I don't believe in body language."

"You… don't believe in it?"

"No. If I am saying something, I say it. My arms don't get a vote."

Arthur inhaled deeply. "Martha, body language always communicates. You can say, 'I am happy,' but if your face looks like thunder…"

"That just means I am concentrating," she replied quickly.

"You can say, 'I am listening,' but if you're turned away…"

"That means I am listening from a distance," she said with determination.

"And if you are scowling while telling someone they are valued…"

"That just means I am serious," she said bluntly.

Arthur paused. "Martha… your body language is revealing your true emotions."

She gasped. "It is betraying me?!"

Before Arthur could answer, Lancelot strutted back past the doorway, having taken Morag for a lovely cup of fine tea: chest puffed, hair gleaming in an entirely unnecessary breeze.

Martha observed him. "See, now he has terrible body language. Look at him, strutting about. No wonder he has so many girlfriends."

Arthur's jaw twitched. "Focus, Martha."

Arthur summoned a group of knights and maids to the chamber holding the Round Table. "We will now practise body language."

Martha folded her arms. "I don't like this. My arms don't know what they're doing unless I tell them."

"Precisely," Arthur replied. "That is what we are here to fix."

He gestured to Gawain. "Gawain is going to say the phrase, 'I am very pleased with your work.' But he will do it with different body language. You must interpret what he really means."

Gawain stepped forward. He cleared his throat. He stood, arms crossed, chin tucked, and eyes narrowed. "I am *very pleased* with your work."

Martha clapped. "Oh! He loves it!"

Arthur stared in disbelief. "Martha… what about that looked positive?"

"Well, he said it."

"But what about his body language?!" Arthur exclaimed, as if in anguish.

Martha interrupted. "He's probably just a bit cold."

Arthur looked up at the ceiling as if appealing to the gods. "Gawain, again," he commanded.

This time Gawain stomped towards Martha, jabbed a finger aggressively in her direction and snarled "I am very pleased with your work!"

Martha gasped. "Oh no! He's furious!"

Arthur nodded. "Yes! The body language and tone contradicted the words."

Martha frowned. "Then why did he say it like that?"

"Because that's the point!" Arthur replied, looking towards the heavens again.

"Well, that's silly," Martha snorted back.

Arthur closed his eyes to regain his composure. When he was finally ready, he opened them. "Let us try it with someone gentler. Percival, please demonstrate a warm, welcoming posture."

Percival stepped forward, softened his shoulders, opened his arms, smiled warmly. "I am very pleased with your work," he said gently.

Martha recoiled from the advancing Percival. "AAAAH!"

Arthur jumped in. "Martha, what's wrong?!"

"He's coming in for a hug! I *hate* surprise hugs! They're dangerous!"

Percival froze. "I was merely…"

"Don't you touch me!" she snapped, waving her mop like a defensive weapon.

Percival backed away, arms raised.

Arthur intervened quickly. "Martha! He was demonstrating openness!"

"So *why* were his arms so wide? That's attack mode!"

"That is *welcome mode*, Martha."

Martha frowned. "Attack mode. Welcome mode. Very similar."

Arthur almost screamed. Tristan, having observed the rather distressing scene, came in with a lovely cup of camomile tea for Arthur. Arthur thanked Tristan with a warm smile, placed a hand on his shoulder, and accepted the tea, demonstrating through his body language that he appreciated Tristan's kind gesture.

"Martha. Different people communicate in different styles. Some direct. Some indirect. Some detailed. Some simple."

Martha nodded thoughtfully. "Oh yes. Morag talks in long sentences. Cissy talks in short sentences. Gawain talks in threats. Lancelot talks in compliments. I talk in truth."

Arthur winced. "Yes... that is one way to describe it."

He pressed the ruby once more on his sword and it glowed again, magically projecting the following styles of communication. Slowly, he read them aloud for Martha to take in:

## COMMUNICATION STYLES

**Direct:** clear, concise, straightforward
**Indirect:** gentle hints, suggestions
**Analytical:** detailed, logical
**Emotional:** expressive, enthusiastic
**Passive:** hesitant, soft
**Assertive:** firm, confident
**Aggressive:** shouting with spoons and sticks

Martha peered at the last one. "Aggressive communication? That one is very me."

Arthur sighed. "Yes. I know."

She beamed proudly. "See? I am on your list."

Just then, panicked footsteps thundered down the hallway. A knight burst into the room, helmet askew, chest heaving. "My lord! We have a problem!"

Arthur stood immediately. "What is it?

"It is the kitchens, sire! There's chaos!"

Arthur turned slowly towards Martha.

Martha shrugged. "What did I do this time? I've not been down there since early this morning."

The knight continued: "The cooks are refusing to cook! The maids are refusing to clean! The fire will not stay lit! And someone said something about a goat being slaughtered, so now there is a goat in the pantry, screaming for help! Or at least I think it is..."

Arthur blinked.

Martha blinked.

"The goat is... very upset, my lord."

Martha frowned. "Well, someone must have misunderstood the instructions."

Arthur gave her a look that could have boiled the moat.

Arthur and Martha rushed down to the kitchens. The scene was explosive, as I am sure you can imagine. Morag was shouting at Cissy. Cissy was shouting at the broom, mop, and bucket. The broom lay broken in half. A pot of something was on fire. A goat was on the table. A cook was crying into a cabbage. Smoke was everywhere. A maid was repeatedly yelling "I THOUGHT YOU SAID *COAT*, NOT *GOAT*!"

Arthur held up his hands. "SILENCE, PLEASE!"

No one stopped. He shouted louder. "**EVERYONE STOP TALKING**!"

Everyone froze instantly. Even the goat. Arthur turned to Martha slowly. "What message did you give your team this morning?"

Martha thought deeply. "Well... I said, 'Right, you lot, get a goat and get cooking'."

Arthur blinked. "You said *'goat'*."

"Yes. For a special stew," she said, nodding.

Arthur exhaled. "Martha... yesterday you said you wanted to stop serving goat."

"I changed my mind."

"And did you check they understood you?"

"No."

"Did you explain where to get the goat?"

"No."

"Did you confirm who was responsible for the goat?"

"No."

"Did you write it down clearly for anyone?"

"I tried! But Morag fainted. She does that a lot, you know. Maybe she is pregnant!"

Arthur brushed a hand over his face. "Martha… let me show you where this went wrong."

Arthur raised Excalibur high. The ruby glowed, spun, and cast a swirling golden vortex against the wall. The image sharpened, as though someone had aimed a celestial projector directly at the past. "Observe," Arthur said gravely, "the precise moment where everything went wrong." The magical recording began to play.

# SCENE 1: MARTHA'S VAGUE INSTRUCTION

There stood Martha, early that morning, pacing in front of her team with all the confidence and clarity of a foghorn in a thunderstorm. She waved a ladle like a royal sceptre. "Right, you lot!" she barked. "Get a goat and get cooking!" She did not point to a goat. In fact, she pointed the ladle towards the coat rack. She did not specify *which* goat. She did not clarify *why* a goat. She merely strode off, muttering something about stew and destiny.

Present Martha winced. "I sounded bossy."

Arthur said nothing, because that was the least of her problems.

## SCENE 2: CISSY MISHEARS THE MESSAGE

The replay zoomed in on Cissy, who stood blinking slowly, as if her brain were buffering. "Did she say... *coat*?" Cissy whispered.

"I think so. I heard 'coat', and she pointed at the coat rack," said the maid who had been yelling earlier.

Morag frowned. "No, she said goat. Definitely goat."

"I also heard coat," another cook piped up.

"I heard oat," said another. "Just oats. Only oats."

"I heard smote," muttered Alice, looking terrified.

"I heard note," said another maid, "and I don't like notes."

"YOU'RE ALL WRONG!" shouted the yelling maid. "SHE SAID *COAT*!"

Cissy folded her arms. "I knew it. I refuse to believe that woman trusts us with a whole goat. Coat makes more sense."

"WHY WOULD WE COOK A COAT?!" Morag roared.

Cissy shrugged. "I don't know. New recipe, I expect?"

Present Martha muttered. "I should've drawn a picture."

## SCENE 3:
## PANIC, CHAOS, AND A VERY UNHAPPY COAT

Back in the projection Alice began running in circles. "What do we do?! Do we slaughter it?! Do we boil it?! Do we negotiate with it?!"

"NO ONE IS NEGOTIATING WITH THE GOAT!" Morag shouted.

"Why not? Goats negotiate all the time," Alice insisted.

"With whom?!" Morag demanded.

Alice paused. "…Other goats?"

Meanwhile, the yelling maid rummaged through the winter coats. "FOUND IT!" she yelled. "We can use this fluffy one for the stew!"

Morag screamed as the maid shoved a coat into the pot.

## SCENE 4:
## THE GOAT ESCAPES

The projection shifted dramatically to the pantry door. The goat: a large, stubborn, wide-eyed creature named Barnaby (though no one had ever bothered to ask) had been minding his own business until three cooks burst in holding a rope, a sack, and a very unconvincing apology. The goat bleated once in protest. Then it bolted. Straight past the cooks. Through the pantry. Under two stools. Between Morag's legs. Over and onto a table. And then into a cupboard, slamming the door behind itself with surprising dignity. Everyone screamed. Cissy fell over. Morag fainted yet again. The pot, coat, and all exploded. Alice threw flour into the air for no reason at all.

# SCENE 5:
# TOTAL, UTTER CARNAGE

The replay widened to show the kitchen in complete meltdown. A broom snapped itself in half in an attempt at self-preservation. A bucket spilled, and the mop slid out. A goose joined the chaos (no one knew where it came from).

One maid shouted, "STEW THE COAT!"

Another shouted, "STOP THE GOAT!"

Someone else yelled, "STEW WHAT?!"

Then someone yelled, "SUE IT!"

The goat came back in and defiantly headbutted a barrel, then leapt onto the table. The barrel rolled into Cissy. Cissy screamed. Martha walked past humming, blissfully unaware, as she went off for her lesson with Arthur, while another cook sat in the corner crying into a cabbage.

Present Martha slapped her own forehead. "Oh, that looks *terrible*."

Arthur paused the projection dramatically. "There," he said, pointing to the frozen image of the goat mid-headbutt, flour hanging in the air like festive snow. "Noise. Ambiguity. No confirmation. No structure. Complete communication collapse."

Present Martha nodded slowly. "Aye. And very messy."

Arthur lowered his sword. "This is why clarity matters, Martha."

She sighed. "Well… at least the goat did not win."

Arthur raised an eyebrow. "Martha, the goat absolutely won."

Martha nodded slowly. "I see it now. It wasn't the goat's fault."

"No, Martha. It was yours."

Martha sighed deeply. "Well. At least it wasn't the mop that self-destructed this time."

The mop, in the vision, immediately snapped in half above them. She glanced at the projection. "…Coward."

Arthur inhaled as the kitchen came back to present time and the projection vanished. "Time to teach you the Communication Cycle."

The goat had finally stopped bleating. Or had given up on life entirely. Either way, the kitchen was now quiet.

Arthur turned to Martha with the solemnity of a man about to address a serious matter and the despair of a man who knew she would misunderstand at least three things before they got through the next five minutes. "Martha," Arthur said, "we must learn the Communication Cycle."

Martha squinted. "Does that involve wheels?"

"No," he said.

"Turning?" she asked.

"No," he said.

"Is it like a waterwheel but for talking?" she asked.

"No!" he snapped, growing more agitated by the second. Arthur drew a circle in the air with his sword. Golden light followed it, forming a glowing loop.

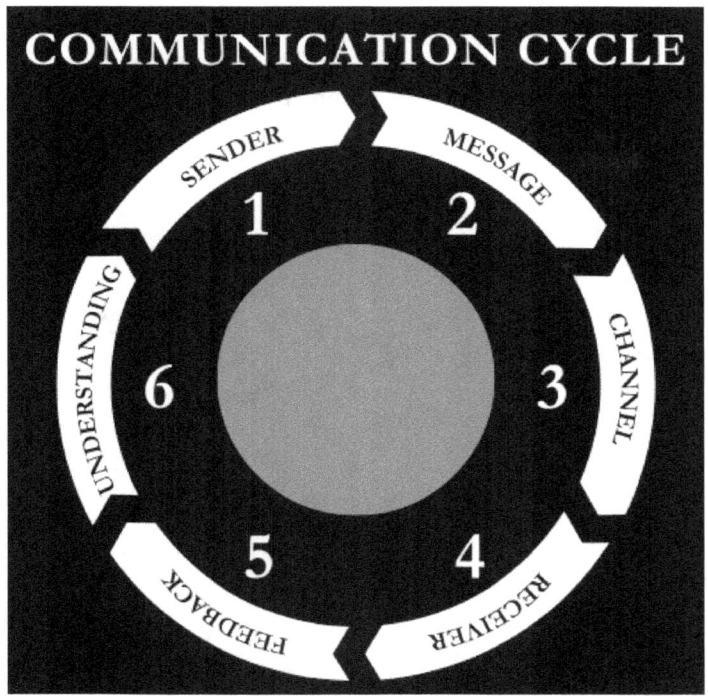

**COMMUNICATION CYCLE**

SENDER 1
MESSAGE 2
CHANNEL 3
RECEIVER 4
FEEDBACK 5
UNDERSTANDING 6

Martha nodded. "Looks like the soup from earlier, but a bit different. Maybe a pie."

Arthur exhaled. "It is not a pie."

"Well, it *could* be a pie."

"It is not a pie, Martha."

"Then someone should fix that."

Arthur ignored her completely. "Let us break it down," he said:

## 1. Sender

"That's the person delivering the message," Arthur explained.

"Me!" Martha said proudly.

Arthur nodded. "Yes. Unfortunately."

## 2. Message

Arthur gave her a stern look. "This must be clear."

Martha nodded. "So, if I say, 'Bring the thing from the place...'?"

Arthur shook his head so violently he nearly decapitated a hanging ladle. "No! That is the opposite of clear."

## 3. Channel

"Spoken voice, written message, *messenger boy*," he said, spitting out the last one as if it had personally offended him.

"Or shouting out of the window!" she replied.

"If you must," he said. "Only if it is the only way."

## 4. Receiver

"Is the person getting the message," he continued.

Martha frowned. "But the problem is, I cannot control what they think."

Arthur paused. "That is... actually very true."

Martha gasped. "I am right?!"

"Yes." Arthur said reluctantly. "But you can make the message easier to understand."

"Oh," she muttered, "less exciting."

## 5. Feedback

"Feedback tells you whether they understood," Arthur said rather proudly.

"Ah yes," Martha said confidently, "when they look confused, leave the room, or wander off muttering, 'I don't get paid enough for this'."

Arthur stared. "No. That is *negative* feedback."

Martha blinked. "What's positive feedback?"

"When someone repeats the message correctly back to you."

Martha frowned. "They never do that."

Arthur sighed.

## 6. Understanding

"This is where you check they got it right," he said, tapping his index finger on the table.

Martha pumped her fist triumphantly. "Yes! I can do that. Easy." She tapped her finger on the table as well.

Arthur hesitated. "Good. Because you've never done it before."

Martha nodded proudly. "Time to start today!"

"Martha," Arthur added, "communication is not only speaking. It is listening as well."

Martha looked horrified. "I *hate* listening."

"You must learn."

"But listening means someone else is talking!"

"That is generally how it works."

"How can I talk if they're talking?!"

"You do not talk if they are talking, or if I am talking."

Martha gasped. "Arthur, that is very unnatural. My mother is Spanish, you know."

He breathed deeply. "Active listening is vital. Watch me." He approached Cissy, who was shaking flour from her hair. "Cissy," Arthur said kindly, "tell me what happened this morning."

Cissy sniffed. "Well… me and a maid heard Martha say 'coat'…"

Arthur nodded. "Yes. Then what happened?"

"Well, Morag heard 'goat', so she panicked. Then the goat panicked. Then we all panicked."

"And how did that make you feel?"

Cissy blinked. "Oh. You actually care?"

"Yes," he said, looking attentively at her.

Cissy softened. "Well... it made me feel a bit... overwhelmed."

"Thank you, Cissy," Arthur said warmly.

Martha watched, eyes narrowed. "That's it?" she asked. "That's 'active listening'?"

"Yes."

"No shouting?"

"No."

"No interrupting?"

"No."

"No poking her with sticks?"

"No!"

Martha folded her arms. "This is going to be harder than I imagined."

Arthur gestured to Morag. "Martha, try with Morag."

Martha inhaled. "I can do this." She approached Morag gently. "Morag," she said in a slow, soothing tone, "tell me what happened."

Morag opened her mouth to speak.

Martha immediately interrupted. "WAIT! I am listening! GO!"

Morag blinked. "Well... I thought you said..."

Martha interrupted again. "I hear you. Continue."

Morag tried again. "So, then I..."

"Yes. I am listening very hard. Harder than anyone has ever listened," Martha cut in again.

Morag hesitated.

Martha leaned forward aggressively, her face two inches from Morag's. "I am listening so much right now."

Morag shrank back. "I feel very uncomfortable."

"Good!" Martha barked. "That means it is working!"

Arthur ran forward. "Martha! STOP! That is not active listening. That is... Active Intimidation!"

Martha stepped back. "Oh. Easy mistake."

"No," Arthur said. "It is not an easy mistake."

At that moment, a loud crash echoed from upstairs.

A knight ran into the kitchen, breathless. "MY LORD! THE ROUND TABLE... IT IS BROKEN!" he screeched at the top of his voice.

Arthur's eyes widened. "How?!"

"Someone misheard an instruction!" the knight said, calming down a little.

Arthur paled. "What instruction?"

The knight gulped. "Someone said, 'Polish the Round Table.' But they misheard it as, 'Demolish the Round Table.' And... well..."

Martha gasped. "That table is a national treasure!"

Arthur turned slowly to face her. "Martha. This is your fault."

Martha nodded sadly. "Yes. Yes, it is."

Arthur pointed at her firmly. "You caused this through unclear instruction. Now *you* will fix it, with proper communication."

Martha took a deep breath. This was her moment. Her opportunity. Her chance to use every piece of learning from Arthur's second lesson. She squared her shoulders. "RIGHT!" she shouted. "No, wait. Calm. Calm voice. Using the right channel. Professional."

Arthur nodded encouragingly. Martha walked towards the knights. "Everyone," she said clearly, "we need to repair the Round Table. Here are your instructions."

She proceeded slowly, following the Communication Cycle:

1. **Sender:** She stood confidently in the centre of them all.
2. **Message:** "We are repairing the Round Table. Not breaking anything else."
3. **Channel:** Clear voice. Calm tone.
4. **Receiver:** She looked at each knight individually, making eye contact with each in turn.
5. **Feedback:** "Please repeat the instructions back to me so I can check our understanding." The knights repeated them perfectly. "We will repair the Round Table and not break anything else," they chimed together.
6. **Understanding:** She nodded. "Good. Now let us make a start."

Arthur watched with genuine pride as each knight took their place. No one shouted. No one panicked. No one introduced livestock into the situation. Within minutes, the Round Table was restored. Without a goat in sight.

Arthur raised his sword again as **Mehrabian** and **Shannon-Weaver** returned dramatically. The two theories appeared on the wall like heroic champions.

# ALBERT MEHRABIAN
# TONE & BODY LANGUAGE

Martha nodded. "Right. No shouting. No waving spoons. No angry eyebrows unless absolutely necessary."

# SHANNON–WEAVER COMMUNICATION CYCLE

Martha nodded hard and shouted. "SENDER, MESSAGE, CHANNEL, RECEIVER, FEEDBACK, UNDERSTANDING. I HAVE GOT IT!"

Arthur beamed. "Martha, you have passed today's training."

Martha gasped delightedly. "I did it?!"

"Yes."

She pumped her fist in the air. "Communication queen I am!"

Arthur frowned. "We will... work on the titles," he said, placing a hand on her shoulder. "Martha, next week you will learn a skill just as important."

She leaned in eagerly. "What is it?"

Arthur smiled faintly. "Delegation."

Martha gasped. "Oh! I already do that! I delegate everything!"

Arthur winced. "Yes. That is exactly why we need to talk."

Cissy ran in, looking panicked. "Miss Martha! The goat has escaped and gone outside to the vegetable patch!"

Martha sighed. "Well... someone needs to go and get it, Cissy."

Arthur raised a finger. "Martha... how will you communicate that instruction?"

Martha straightened. "Right. Cissy," she said calmly, "please retrieve the goat, Barnaby, safely from the vegetable patch. And can you tell me what I have asked you to do, and which goat needs getting?"

Cissy nodded. "You want me to fetch the white goat with the brown patch over his left eye, near the vegetable patch, called Barnaby."

Martha beamed. "Yes, that's exactly right. And when you've done it, we can all have some cherry pie!"

Cissy ran off. "Cherry pie for me!" she called as she left the room. A moment later, Cissy shouted through the open window. "What if it has moved to the other side of the garden and is by the fruit trees now?!"

Martha groaned.

Arthur sighed.

And the lesson ended there, until next week.

# CHAPTER THREE

## Trust, Control, and
## Doing It Yourself Anyway
### Delegation, Trust & Engagement

The morning sun drifted over Camelot like a gentle reminder from the universe that time stops for no one, not even for Martha, who was currently lying face-down on a kitchen bench, one foot twitching occasionally like a sleeping horse. The kitchen was... surprisingly tidy. Not perfect, but tidier than usual. This was because Martha, in a burst of misguided productivity the night before, had cleaned half the kitchen herself, shouting the entire time, "IF YOU WANT SOMETHING DONE PROPERLY, YOU MIGHT AS WELL DO IT YOURSELF!" This was, ironically, the opposite of today's lesson.

Arthur stepped into the Grand Hall, preparing himself mentally for Martha and Week Three of training. He had meditated at dawn. He had bathed in cold water. He had done breathing exercises. He had even tried chanting. None of it, though, would be enough.

Right on cue, Martha stumbled in, hair wild, apron inside-out, clutching a bucket in one hand and a mop in the other like a pair of defeated warriors. "Morning, Arthur," she croaked. "I have been up since three."

Arthur stared. "Why?"

"Had to clean the whole kitchen. Fired the staff for being lazy yesterday. Then rehired them this morning, because cleaning everything was awful."

Arthur blinked. "You fired and rehired your staff over the same night?"

Martha nodded. "Aye. Not just once actually, but twice."

Arthur pinched the bridge of his nose, a very familiar sight when Martha was around. "Sit," he said gently. "Today's lesson is all about delegation."

Martha dropped into the chair like a sack of potatoes falling down a well.

"Now, Martha," Arthur began carefully, "tell me why you cleaned the whole kitchen alone."

"Because everyone else is so damn useless."

Arthur raised an eyebrow. "Everyone?"

Martha hesitated. "Well… everyone except Morag. She's only mostly useless."

"And Cissy?" he enquired.

Martha scoffed. "She tries. But she cries too much."

"And the other cooks and maids?"

"They all breathe too loudly, if you know what I mean," she replied thoughtfully.

Arthur inhaled. "Right. I see the problem."

Martha leaned in eagerly. "So, today you'll teach me how to get them all to work harder?"

"No," Arthur said firmly. "Today I will teach you how not to do everything yourself."

Martha frowned. "But if I don't do it myself, how will it be right?"

Arthur smiled patiently. "Martha… that is something called lack of trust."

She gasped. "I trust them! I trust they will mess it up, I trust they will get it wrong every single time!"

"That," Arthur said, "is not the type of trust I am talking about." Arthur lifted his sword. The ruby pulsed, and the remote once again got to work. "Martha," he said, "today's experts are two future-wise men named **Ken Blanchard and Paul Hersey**, who will teach something called Situational Leadership."

The glowing words appeared on the wall:

**'People need different levels of direction and support depending on their skills and confidence.'**

Martha squinted. "So, they are going to be saying in years to come that different people need different things?"

"Yes, that's right. That's *exactly* what they will say," Arthur said, nodding his head with great exaggeration.

Martha went on and posed a multiple question to Arthur. "Like Lancelot needs praise? Gawain needs armour polish? And Cissy needs tissues?"

"…Surprisingly accurate," he replied.

She puffed up proudly, her arms firmly crossed beneath her chest.

Arthur continued. "You cannot take one approach with your entire team. You must delegate based on their capability and willingness."

Martha frowned. "Isn't capability just willingness with more steps?"

"No. Capability is skill. Willingness is motivation."

Martha blinked. "I am getting confused."

Arthur sighed and decided, at this point, to just move on. He picked up a stack of large wooden spoons and handed all of them to Martha at once.

Martha staggered backwards under the weight. "Arthur! They are very heavy!"

"Exactly," he said. "This is called dumping, giving tasks with no support at all." He took them back. Then gave her just two spoons. "This," he said, "is like delegation. It is assigning a task that clearly matches the skill, capability and capacity of the individual without overloading them, but giving them enough of a challenge."

Martha nodded. "I like delegation. I can handle the two spoons, but dumping that lot on me, not so much."

"Good," Arthur said. "Because you have been doing a lot of dumping."

Martha looked offended. "I have *not*!"

Arthur raised an eyebrow. "You told Cissy to polish the armour, all 183 pieces, alone, and all before breakfast."

"She's young!" Martha protested.

"She had to have a lie down afterwards," exclaimed Arthur.

"Well, she should build herself some stamina," Martha retorted with ease.

Arthur stared. "That is not how stamina works."

Arthur guided Martha to stand in front of the Round Table. "Trust," he said, "is believing others can do good work."

Martha folded her arms. "But what if they cannot?"

Arthur smiled. "Then you teach them. You do not take the work away."

Martha blinked. "So… if they cannot do something, I am supposed to help them until they can?"

"Yes, that's right. Exactly right. Well done!"

"And… not shout at them?" she carried on.

"Correct. No shouting. Shouting is not needed," he said, his voice quickening with each answer.

Martha sighed. "That sounds exhausting."

"Not as exhausting as doing everything yourself," Arthur said quietly.

Martha paused. "…That's a fair point."

Arthur raised his ruby sword and a new glowing light appeared on the wall:

## EMPOWERMENT
'Giving people the authority, confidence, and resources to succeed.'

Martha squinted. "So... letting them do the job... and trusting them to do it... and giving them what they need... makes them better?"

"Yes."

"And it makes my life easier?"

"Yes."

Martha gasped. "Arthur... are you telling me I have been making more work for myself all this time?!"

Arthur nodded gently. "Yes, Martha."

Martha threw her head back. "Why did no one tell me?!"

Arthur's eyelid twitched. "I have. Several times."

"I guess I wasn't listening!" she said, looking directly at him.

"Yes. That is also part of the problem," he said as he turned away. "Let me show you something else to help you understand." Arthur raised his sword once more. "Let us review how you delegated and empowered last week."

The projection flickered to life across the ceiling. Craning her neck upwards to see it, the projection came to life.

Projected Martha stood in the kitchen, waving her spoon. Her apron flapped behind her like a tattered battle flag. Her hair was pinned up with a fork. Her ladle, her self-declared 'Leadership Baton', was clutched in one tight fist. The cooks and maids were huddled around a chopping block, trying to look busy in that hopeful, doomed way of people praying not to be noticed. Martha did not share their intention. Martha swooped into the centre of the room, raised her ladle like Moses parting the Red Sea, and declared: "Right! Listen up, team! We're going to be productive today!"

Cissy jumped. Morag dropped an onion. Alice ran into a shelf. Martha began pacing back and forth, flicking the spoon in every direction as though conducting an orchestra that did not appreciate being conducted.

"You!" she barked at a maid who hadn't done anything wrong yet. "Do something!"

The maid blinked. "Something like... what, Miss Martha?"

"HOW WOULD I KNOW?!" Martha roared. "USE YOUR INITIATIVE!"

The maid panicked and began polishing a carrot with her apron. Martha whirled around. "YOU!" she pointed at Alice. "DO SOMETHING ELSE!"

Alice froze mid-breath. "What else, Miss Martha?"

"ANYTHING ELSE, JUST NOT THAT!" Martha boomed back.

Alice grabbed a pot, the wrong pot, as later events would reveal, and began stirring it with frantic enthusiasm.

Martha marched towards Cissy, who was trying desperately to look invisible. "You!" Martha snapped. "Stop crying, like a big baby!"

Cissy hiccupped. "I, I am not crying, Miss."

"WELL, START THEN!" Martha shouted, then immediately changed her mind and barked, "No, stop! No crying in my kitchen!"

Cissy, utterly confused, produced a tear on command anyway.

Martha pivoted back to Alice, who was still enthusiastically stirring the wrong pot. "STOP!" she shouted. "NOT THAT POT! IT'S THIS POT!"

Martha went over to it. She shoved aside a nearby maid and stood by the other pot and stirred it vigorously. "LIKE THIS, DO YOU SEE?!" she yelled at Alice, then suddenly correcting her poor stirring skills. "This is how you stir things up around here!"

Alice, who had not been doing anything wrong in the way she stirred to begin with, only in the wrong pot, stepped closer to the pot that Martha was now stirring. She held up her hands to take the spoon from Martha so she could continue with the stirring of this pot.

"Oh no. Oh no you don't," Martha said. "All of you, just move on out of my kitchen! I will just do it all myself!"

Alice, along with the others, sighed and stepped back, defeated.

Present Martha buried her face in her hands, as Tristan entered the room, carrying some items.

"Oh, that looked bad," Tristan said with a grimace.

Arthur nodded. "It was."

Martha peeked through her fingers. "I am a monster."

Arthur considered. "…Yes. Yes, you are."

The room returned to normal and the vision on the ceiling disappeared slowly, as Tristan placed four items on the table: a broom, a knife, a mixing bowl and a scroll.

"Martha," Arthur said, "I want you to assign each item to a member of our team, but only to someone who is suited for the task."

Martha nodded. She picked up the broom. "Morag!"

Arthur frowned. "And why Morag?"

Martha shrugged. "She hates cleaning."

"That is *not* a reason," he said, dropping his head in disbelief.

She sighed. "Fine. Cissy then."

"Better. But why?"

"Because she needs practice."

"Excellent. You may be getting the hang of this," he said finally, with a smile.

Martha handed the broom to Cissy, who accepted it without crying, a small miracle. Next, Martha picked up the mixing bowl. "Morag!"

Arthur nodded. "Yes. Morag has cooking skills."

Martha beamed. Then she picked up the knife. "Cissy."

Arthur almost fainted. "No! Cissy is terrified of knives!"

"She needs to face her fears!" Martha said, waving the knife at Cissy.

"No, Martha," Arthur said, as he took the knife from Martha. "Delegation is not trauma exposure."

Martha rolled her eyes. "Fine. Morag gets the knife too."

"So, Morag gets the knife and the bowl," he said, handing the knife to Morag whilst checking Martha had meant exactly that.

"Yes, she does," Martha said with ease.

Arthur then looked at the last item on the table, the scroll.

Martha held it up. "…Tristan!"

Arthur paused. "That might actually work. At least he can read," he said, nodding in Tristan's direction.

Martha shrugged. "Plus, he'll look handsome reading it," she said, pursing her lips towards him.

Arthur rubbed his temples and took the scroll from Martha and read it aloud. "Martha, this is a list of tasks for a noon feast today. You must now delegate properly."

Martha inhaled deeply. She stood straight. Calm. Focused. "Morag," she started, "can you please clean and prepare the vegetables and slice them finely? Cissy, could you," she continued, "sweep the floors and tidy the pantry, making sure everything is in its right place." Finally, she turned to Tristan. "Could you please go to the kitchen with the cooks and maids and read the menu aloud to check that we have all the correct ingredients?"

Arthur nodded approvingly.

"And while you all do that, I will sit up here and have a cup of tea." Martha added.

Arthur's jaw dropped. "Martha! That is *not* delegation!"

She smiled innocently. "Empowerment?"

Arthur glared. "No!"

"Worth a try," she said with a wry smile.

Arthur moved and began stretching his back with the weary elegance of a man who had been carrying Camelot on his shoulders for far too long. "Martha," he said, "before we continue on, I think we must focus on trust."

Martha scoffed. "As I said before, I trust everyone. To disappoint me."

Arthur resisted the urge to sigh. "No, Martha. Trust means believing your team can succeed, even if they need training first."

Martha narrowed her eyes. "So, I trust them... even if they're terrible now?"

Arthur nodded. "Yes. Because they might not be terrible forever."

Martha stared off into the distance, imagining a future in which Cissy did not sob into the stew. "That's... a hopeful thought," she said.

Arthur broke her daydream with the clap of his hands. "Knights! Gather!" he said with urgency.

They all entered the room and lined up obediently. Martha stood among them like a suspicious cat among much taller cats in armour.

"We are doing a trust fall," Arthur announced.

Martha frowned. "Trust fall... isn't that when someone falls backwards, and you trust they don't crack their skull open because you did not manage to catch them?"

"More or less."

Martha crossed her arms. "Seems risky to me."

Arthur nodded. "It is. That is the whole point." He gestured towards Lancelot. "Lancelot, will you go first, please."

Lancelot nodded gracefully, stepped forward, and positioned himself in front of the group. He looked over his shoulder, winked at two maids who had suddenly snuck back up the stairway and whispered, "Catch me gently, darlings."

The maids swooned.

"Now," Arthur commanded, "fall."

Lancelot fell back like a fainting poet. The knights and maids caught him effortlessly, lowered him gently, and then all of them applauded his bravery.

Martha snorted. "Show-off."

Arthur turned to Martha. "Your turn."

She froze. "What? No. No, absolutely not."

"Martha," Arthur said gently, "delegation requires trust."

"But I barely trust gravity!"

"Martha," he appealed.

"No! Absolutely not! They will drop me!"

Arthur sighed. "Fine. Then you, on your own, will catch someone. Gawain!"

Gawain stepped forward confidently. He loomed over Martha like a large shelf about to fall. Martha squinted at him. "Gawain... how much armour are you wearing?"

"Standard loadout," Gawain said proudly. "Nine stone of plate, chain, and righteous masculinity."

Martha muttered. "That's too much righteousness for one person."

Arthur stepped back. "Ready?"

Gawain smiled. "I trust you, Martha, I really do!"

As he fell backward, Martha's eyes went wide. She extended her arms. Braced herself. Then suddenly she whispered. "Oh blast." As Gawain fell backwards into her arms, Martha... stepped aside.

"OH NO!" someone screamed. CLANG. Gawain hit the floor with the musical resonance of a dropped cathedral bell.

Arthur closed his eyes. "Martha," he said in despair.

She raised her hands defensively. "He was going to be too heavy! He's like a falling horse!"

Gawain groaned. "My spleen..."

Arthur rubbed his temples. "Martha, you don't step away in a trust fall. You step towards them."

Martha frowned. "That seems counterintuitive."

Arthur looked up at the heavens. "Why me?"

Once Gawain had been rolled to the side (to 'rest'), Arthur continued. "Martha, now let us touch once again on our lesson."

Martha perked up. "Oh yes! That's where I don't do anything, and they do everything!"

Arthur froze. "No. That is abandonment. Not delegation or empowerment."

"Oh," she said, shrugging her shoulders.

"Remember," he said as the ruby started to glow and another vision appeared above them.

> 'EMPOWERMENT is giving people
> the freedom, tools, and accountability
> to do their jobs effectively.'
>
> 'DELEGATION is giving someone the
> responsibility and authority to get
> their jobs done whilst the leader remains
> accountable for their employees' actions.'

Martha shrugged. "I can do that."

Arthur handed her a scroll, as the two maids went back downstairs and the knights left the room. "This is the list of tasks for the lunchtime service today. Go on and empower your team. Do not take over. Do not micromanage. Do not shout. Simply delegate and empower them."

Martha nodded and headed down into the kitchen.

After about ten minutes, a scream erupted. Morag was shouting. "WHY IS THERE A FIRE IN THE SPICE CUPBOARD?!"

Arthur sprinted down the stairs immediately to see what was happening. The scene was... unconventional when he entered the kitchen. Cissy was standing on the square table, wobbling perilously, juggling three onions with the brow-furrowed intensity of someone who had *never* juggled anything in her life.

"What are you doing?!" Arthur cried.

Cissy grinned brightly. "Martha just said I could express my creative freedom! Look!" she said as she threw the onions into the air. One onion arched gracefully through the air and landed in the kitchen sink. Another hit Alice on the forehead at the far end of the room. The third rolled off the table and into the fire. "I call it 'Onionic Expressionism'!" Cissy declared proudly.

Arthur stared in disbelief. "This... is not what empowerment means, Martha."

Cissy grinned harder, lost her balance, and fell backwards into a sack of flour. Meanwhile, Morag was slapping a small fire in the spice cupboard with a large cookbook titled 'Roasts of the Realm'.

"Morag!" Arthur shouted. "What has happened?!"

Morag did not look up. "I tried to make the spices more exciting!"

"With fire?!"

"Well, now they're *very* exciting, but they got a little too hot to handle!" She whacked the flames again with the cookbook. A cloud of paprika burst out like a red fog of doom." Morag coughed. "So much... flavour... nice."

At the far end of the room, Alice and Eve were crouched on the floor, surrounding a shimmering white pile of flour.

"What exactly are you two doing?" Arthur demanded.

Alice looked up, eyes sparkling with manic inspiration. "We're conducting an experiment!"

Eve nodded eagerly. "Martha said we could innovate!"

Arthur's face paled. "What experiment?"

"How flammable is flour... *really*?" Eve whispered reverently.

Arthur screamed. "STOP!"

Too late. Alice struck a spark. A small, dramatic *whoosh* of fire erupted upward, singeing both their eyebrows.

"We have results!" Eve shouted joyfully.

On the other side of the kitchen, one of the maids sat at a table drawing pictures of food instead of preparing any.

She sketched a beautiful bowl of stew, complete with steam curls and floating herbs.

Arthur approached slowly. "…Why are you not making actual stew?"

The maid held up her drawing proudly. "Martha empowered me to follow my passions! And I love drawing stew!"

Arthur exhaled through his nose. "Does the drawing feed anyone?"

"It feeds my soul."

Arthur looked to the heavens. "Why must I suffer?" Finally, Arthur spotted something that made him stop mid-step. A goose strutted across the kitchen floor wearing a tea towel like a cape. Arthur blinked. "…Why is that goose dressed in a tea towel?"

A nearby maid whispered reverently, "Martha said we should empower *all* living beings."

Arthur's jaw dropped. "So, you put a tea towel on a goose?!"

The maid nodded. "She has self-esteem issues."

"How can you possibly know that?!"

The maid shrugged. "She never stands up straight."

Arthur sank to his knees. "This is not empowerment," he whispered. "This is madness."

Martha beamed proudly at the catastrophe. "Look at them, Arthur!" she said triumphantly. "They're empowered!"

Arthur stared at her with hollow eyes. "They're empowered to destroy the kitchen..." He gestured helplessly toward the chaos, "...and possibly the entire castle."

Martha smiled. "And they're doing it all by themselves! Isn't that marvellous?"

Arthur inhaled deeply, preparing his emotionally supportive sigh. "Martha... we need to talk," he said, looking around in horror. "This is not empowerment! *This is anarchy!*"

"But they're doing things!" she said with a smile.

"They're doing the *wrong* things!"

Martha rubbed her chin. "Perhaps I gave them too much freedom."

Arthur nodded vigorously. "Yes! Empowerment needs boundaries!"

Martha sighed. "Fine. Fine. I understand." She picked up a ladle. "Stop whatever you're all doing immediately!"

Arthur snatched the ladle away. "Martha! You cannot switch between chaos and dictatorship! There is a middle ground!"

She folded her arms, looking around the room. "Where?!"

Arthur inhaled. "Right. Time for some more of the **Ken Blanchard** model." Arthur raised his sword, creating another of his glowing diagrams in the air:

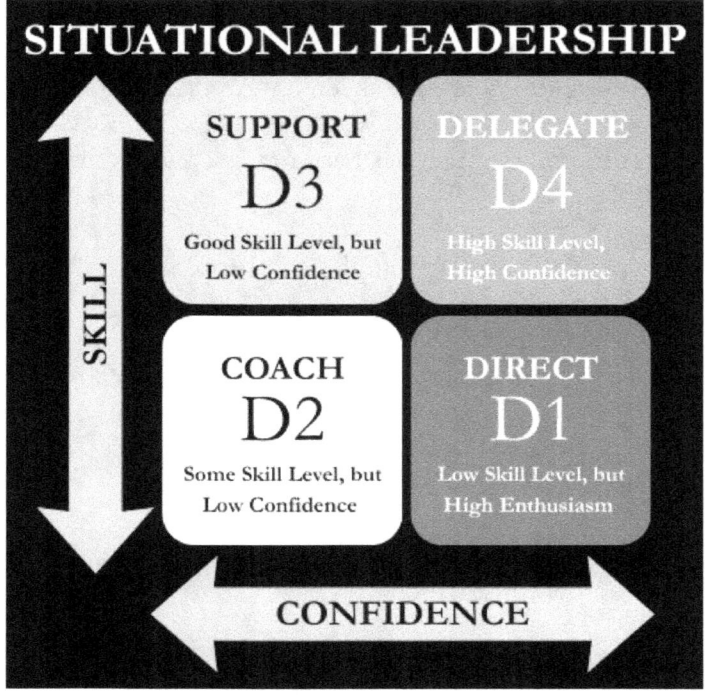

Martha blinked. "What in the name of gravy is that?!"

Arthur pointed. "This tells you who is ready for delegation, and who needs help."

Martha studied the glowing instructions. "Which one is Cissy?"

"D2. She tries hard but lacks confidence," Arthur responded with ease.

Martha nodded. "Yes. Crying category. And Morag?" she asked.

"D4. Skilled and confident," he answered again with ease, as if he knew more about her staff than she did.

"Knife category," Martha sneered. "And Alice?"

Arthur hesitated. Alice was hard to place but, in the end, he said, "…D1."

"Ah yes. The walks-into-apples category," she smiled.

Arthur also smiled. "Exactly. So, you delegate to D4s. You support D3s. You coach D2s. And you direct D1s."

Martha nodded slowly. "Ohhhhh... That's right, delegation… isn't one-size-fits-all."

Arthur exhaled with relief. "Yes! Precisely! You choose based on their readiness!"

Martha raised her eyebrows. "That's so clever."

"Yes, it is, isn't it."

"Shame I did not know this earlier," she added.

Arthur rubbed his temples once again.

Just then, a knight burst into the main kitchen. "MY LORD! THERE'S AN EMERGENCY!"

Arthur braced himself. "What now?"

"The cauldron at the back, near the pantry!" the knight gasped. "It has overflowed! It's flooded the hallway towards the armoury! And someone must've misheard something, because the staff all think they're not allowed to touch it!"

Arthur stared. "Martha?"

Martha bit her lip. "I may have said, 'Don't touch the cauldron... yet.' But I did it in my *do not ever touch* voice."

Arthur groaned. "Martha. Delegation needs clear authority boundaries."

She sighed. "Right. I will fix it."

She turned to Cissy. "Cissy," she said gently, "you're responsible for turning off the cauldron. Tell me what your job is."

Cissy straightened. "I will turn off the cauldron."

"Yes. And if you're unsure how to do that?"

"I will ask Morag," Cissy said, beaming.

"Good. And Morag... what will your job be?"

Morag grinned. "I will keep the cauldron and kitchen safe."

"Yes. And you, Alice..." Martha narrowed her eyes. "Can I trust you not to run into the cauldron? You *will* stay well away from it while the others continue with their duties."

Alice nodded vigorously, already edging backwards.

"Excellent," Arthur said, impressed.

Martha continued delegating. "You two, mop the floor. You, open the windows. You, take the goose out of the tea towel. You, pick up the onions and sweep up the flour."

Finally, the chaos began to settle. The cauldron stopped bubbling over once it was turned off. The floor was mopped and dried. The kitchen and the flooded hallway to the armoury were safe again. Everyone, for once, looked like a functioning team.

Arthur folded his arms. "Martha... that was proper delegation."

Martha smiled slightly. "It felt... good."

"It *is* good."

"It felt like... less work."

"It *is* less work," he said, placing a hand on her shoulder.

She thought deeply. "So, delegation isn't just about getting others to do things. It's about trusting the right people with the right tasks... and giving them what they need."

Arthur smiled warmly. "Yes, Martha."

She nodded proudly. "And not letting Gawain fall on the floor."

Arthur sighed. "Yes. That too."

Arthur stood at the threshold of the kitchen, surveying his newly improved pupil with pride… and caution. Martha's shoulders were finally down instead of up around her ears, which was progress. The kitchen was cleaner than usual, also progress. The goat and goose were nowhere in sight. This was, perhaps, the greatest progress of all. "Martha," Arthur began, "you have demonstrated growth today. You've shown you can delegate. You've built some trust. Now you must do something that is the most terrifying part of any training course."

Martha tensed. "Is it budgeting? I hate budgeting."

"No."

"Performance reviews? They're awkward," she asked.

"No."

"Is it… Human Resources?"

Arthur looked horrified. "Good heavens, no. That field will not be invented for centuries."

Martha sighed in relief. "Then what is it?"

Arthur stepped forward, face solemn. "The Empowerment Challenge."

Martha froze. "Oh. That is terrifying."

Arthur clapped his hands. "Team! Gather!"

The kitchen staff assembled like a mismatched collection of nobility's reject picks. Cissy clutched her broom, still trembling slightly. Morag wielded a knife like she was ready to duel the gods. Alice tried to look competent while standing as far away from the walls as possible.

Arthur addressed them. "Today, Martha will not direct you. She will not take over. She will not shout. She will simply say, 'I trust you to prepare a finger-buffet banquet in the next two hours.' And then she will... leave."

Martha gasped. "*Leave*?!"

"Yes."

"*Leave the room completely*?!" she almost screeched.

"Yes," Arthur said, calmly and clearly.

"*And let them do things unsupervised*?!"

Arthur nodded. "Yes, Martha. If delegation is giving tasks... then empowerment is giving ownership."

Martha clutched her chest. "But I am not ready."

"You are."

"I will faint."

"No, you will not."

"I will vomit."

"Possibly, but that is not relevant," he said with a wry smile.

Martha inhaled shakily. She stepped forward, turned to her staff, and in the quietest voice she had ever used, barely louder than a sigh, said, "I... trust you."

The staff looked at one another in amazement.

Morag stepped forward. "Sorry, what was that? Say it again?"

Martha swallowed. "I trust you. To run my kitchen and prepare a finger-buffet banquet... *without me.*"

The room froze. Cissy dropped her broom. Morag dropped her jaw. Alice dropped a carrot when a rabbit started talking Welsh. The carrot rolled beneath a bench, never to be seen again. Somewhere, a chicken wore a crown, as if preparing for a coronation.

Slowly, reality began to return.

Martha turned to Arthur. "OK, I said it. Can I stay now?"

Arthur took her arm. "No." He dragged her out of the kitchen like a parent removing a child from a sweet shop.

Arthur sat Martha down upstairs at the Round Table. "This is part of the lesson."

Martha's knee bounced. Her fingers twitched. Her left eye developed a nervous flutter. "I cannot do nothing!" she wailed.

"Yes," Arthur said calmly, "you can quite easily do nothing."

"I hate doing nothing!"

"So, I have noticed," he said, with gentle reassurance.

"What if they burn something?!"

"Then they will learn."

"What if they break something?!"

"Then they will grow."

"What if they summon a demon accidentally?!"

Arthur hesitated. "...Unlikely."

Martha buried her face in her hands. "What if... what if they don't need me?"

Arthur smiled gently. "Martha, empowerment is not about making yourself unnecessary. It is about *making them capable*. A leader who empowers others becomes more valuable to an organisation, not less."

Martha peeked through her fingers. "You really think so?"

Arthur nodded. "Yes."

Just then… BOOM. A distant crash echoed through the castle.

Arthur shot to his feet. "What now?"

Footsteps thundered towards the Hall. A knight burst in, panting. "My lord! The central hearth is blocked! Smoke is flooding the rooms and hallways!"

Arthur gasped. "That hearth heats half the castle! Someone must clear the flue at once!"

The knight nodded. "Yes, sire! But everyone is arguing in the courtyard about who should lead the repair team."

Arthur whirled to face Martha. "*This*… is your moment."

Martha stiffened. "You want me to fix the hearth in the hallway now?"

"No," Arthur said. "I know you want to do it. But this is a time to delegate." He pointed towards the courtyard. "My knights must solve this. You must lead them, not do it for them."

Martha inhaled. Her spine straightened. Her shoulders squared. She marched towards the window like a woman ready to fight smoke itself. "Knights!" she called into the courtyard. "There is a castle emergency! Please stop arguing and come in here immediately. The hearth flue is blocked, and the whole place is filling with smoke!"

The knights ran into the hallway and clustered near the central hearth.

Tristan snapped to attention. "How bad is it?"

"Bad," said Martha.

"Listen carefully, everyone. Lancelot, you take charge of a cleaning crew. You're my D4: highest skill and highest confidence."

Lancelot beamed.

"Tristan, you're with him. You're D2. You need support, not orders."

Tristan nodded bravely.

"Gawain, you stay here and rest after your fall from earlier."

Gawain saluted. "Yes, indeed, Martha!"

"Percival, gather all tools needed and report to Lancelot."

"Yes, Martha!"

Martha carried on, now in full swing. "Ector, fetch water. Galahad, grab old bed sheets or blankets for the soot."

"Yes!" they both shouted, exiting stage left, followed by the Goose.

Martha turned back. Everyone looked energised, organised and focused. She swallowed. "Right on," she said, far too loudly.

The team moved like an army of very determined ants.

Martha stood still, trembling slightly.

Arthur appeared behind her. "You did not take over and do it all," he said.

Martha nodded. "I delegated."

"You did nothing but give out the instructions. You trusted them," he said, smiling.

"I have," she said, watching intently.

"And now look," Arthur added, grinning so broadly it almost counted as a miracle.

Minutes later, the knights finished up, triumphant.

Lancelot stepped forward. "Flue is clear!" he reported.

Gawain added, "And no one fell down the chimney. So, no more injuries."

Percival puffed up. "And all equipment is returned to the cupboards!"

Martha gasped, clutching her chest in relief. "You all... did it."

Galahad smiled. "You trusted us. We did not want to let you down."

Lancelot nodded. "It feels good being trusted like that."

Tristan added, "And needed in a time of crisis, rather than always in battle."

Martha wiped her eyes discreetly. "Thank you. All of you."

Back at the Round Table, Arthur raised his sword one final time. Glowing words appeared:

## DELEGATION - TRUST - EMPOWERMENT

**Delegate tasks based on skill and readiness.**

**Trust your team: teach, support, and believe in them.**

**Empower them with tools, authority, and confidence.**

Arthur lowered the sword. "Martha, today you have become a leader."

She blinked. "Really?"

"Yes," he said, with real pride in her achievements.

"Really. A proper leader of people like you?"

Arthur coughed. "Erm… let us not push it."

Arthur placed a hand on her shoulder as the cooks and maids came up the stairs from the kitchens below, carrying the finest finger-buffet banquet the castle had ever seen, at least, not since the last head cook died choking on an apple. The knights joined them to enjoy the feast, and Arthur insisted the cooks and maids ate with them too.

Taking Martha aside, he said, "Next week, we will look at Time Management and Prioritisation."

Martha gasped. "Oh dear. I am terrible with time," she said, munching on a Coronation Chicken sandwich which, one day, she felt, would be a right royal hit.

Arthur smiled. "I know," he said, savouring a bite of Welsh rarebit.

# CHAPTER FOUR

## Urgent, Important, and Completely Avoided
Time Management & Prioritisation

The church bells of Camelot chimed. Had time been invented, then they would have been chiming the hour of nine in their usual melodious fashion, which was ironic, because Martha was already three hours behind schedule. At least, according to the schedule she had written the night before. Well... 'written' was being generous. It was more of a diagram. A swirling, looping mess of arrows, circles, stars, and a drawing of a donkey wearing a floppy hat. In the middle, in big letters, she had written: *'DO EVERYTHING TODAY.'*

Arthur had called this training session for sunrise. But sunrise had come and gone. And so had breakfast, as had elevenses. Finally, Martha arrived at the Grand Hall breathlessly, apron flapping, hair wild, carrying three baskets, two buckets, and a pickaxe.

Arthur blinked. "Martha... why do you have a pickaxe?"

She dumped everything onto the Round Table. "Because," she gasped, "the whole of today has been... a *day*."

Arthur raised an eyebrow. "It is only nearly lunchtime."

"Exactly!" Martha snapped. "I have been to the gardens, the stables, the vegetable patch, the market, the armoury, *and* the poorhouses!"

Arthur stared. "...Why?"

"Because everyone needed me!" she said, putting her hand on her heart.

He folded his arms. "Did they?"

"Yes! Morag needed carrots for a stew. Cissy needed hay for the donkey, I think it is a donkey it was wearing a floppy hat. Might be a very large dog. Guinevere needed flowers for her bedroom. The knives needed sharpening. The villagers needed bread, and the pig in the stables needed cheering up!"

Arthur blinked. "Martha... pigs don't need cheering up."

"This one did!" she insisted. "He was melancholy and off his food."

Arthur let out a slow breath. "Martha... do you know what today's lesson is?"

Martha dropped into a chair. "Time management," she wheezed. "And I am terrible at it."

"Yes," Arthur agreed gently. "Yes, you are."

Arthur stood and gestured for Martha to follow him. "Come," he said, "let us start at the beginning. Show me what happened."

They walked outside to the royal gardens, or rather, what was left of them. Flowers were uprooted. Barrows overturned. A gardener stood with his head in his hands.

Martha pointed. "Well, that wasn't my fault. Guinevere said she needed flowers urgently."

The gardener groaned. "But she just wanted a small quality bouquet. Not *all* of them."

Martha shrugged. "She said 'a bouquet worthy of a queen'. I thought that meant quantity."

Arthur rubbed his temples. "Martha... quantity and quality are just as different as urgency and importance. Whilst Guinevere is important, the need really wasn't urgent."

She squinted. "Nope, I don't see it. What's the difference?"

Arthur inhaled. "We will get to that."

They then took a brisk walk to the bustling Camelot marketplace, where traders were yelling. Children were running. A goat was biting someone's trousers. (Arthur suspected it was Barnaby the goat.)

A baker ran up to Martha in a fury. "YOU!" he shouted. "You promised to help with the bread delivery!"

Martha scoffed. "I did not promise anything!"

He held up her schedule, the swirling mess of arrows and doodles. "In this scribble, you gave me: 'Bread delivery, at dawn'."

Martha snatched it. "Oh! I did not know that's what that meant."

Arthur sighed. "You wrote it."

"Yes, but not in my morning writing voice. That was my evening writing voice."

Arthur stared. "Martha… what does that even mean?"

Martha shrugged helplessly. "I don't know any more."

Totally flabbergasted, Arthur decided it was time they headed back to the castle.

Back inside, they passed a housemaid scrubbing the same patch of floor repeatedly over and over again, whilst plucking a goose, folding laundry into a basket, and holding the end of what could only be imagined was a chimney-sweep broom between her teeth.

"Why is she doing that?" Arthur asked.

Martha frowned. "I told her to clean the floors, fetch the laundry, sweep the chimney, and pluck the goose."

Arthur blinked. "*All* of that?"

"Yes."

"At the *same* time?" he said in despair.

Martha nodded. "I told her to multitask. She's been trying to do all four at once for the last hour."

The maid, overhearing this, dropped the chimney-sweep broom from her teeth, stood, and tried to curtsey while holding a half-plucked goose, whilst now using her foot to scrub the floor.

Arthur closed his eyes. "Martha... humans cannot multitask in this way."

"Well, I told her," Martha protested. "She must be doing it wrong."

Arthur breathed deeply. "We have much to learn."

Arthur drew Excalibur and the ruby began to shine, lighting up the wall and producing four clear instructions glowing under the banner 'The Eisenhower Matrix':

## EISENHOWER MATRIX
### Do First, Do Next, Delegate, Delete

Martha squinted. "Is it a code?"

"No."

"A spell?"

"No."

"A mantra?"

"No, Martha."

He pointed to each word and explained how they worked alongside things that are important or urgent. As he pointed, more words appeared in front of them.

"Do First," he said, "things that are both important and urgent."

"Do Next, or schedule it, if it is important, but it is not urgent right now."

"Delegate anything that is not important but might be urgent."

"And Delete it, or don't do it, if it is not important and not urgent."

Martha stared. "So, the flowers…?"

"Well, it is important to Guinevere, but certainly not urgent. It could have been scheduled for later today," he replied.

"And the bread…?"

"Now that was important, and rather urgent to get everyone fed for breakfast."

"And the pig cheering-up…"

Arthur pinched the bridge of his nose. "Definitely not important and definitely not urgent. Not necessary. Not even sane."

Martha nodded slowly. "This is… helpful."

Arthur smiled. "Good."

Arthur and Martha stood beneath a new shimmering projection of the Eisenhower Matrix.

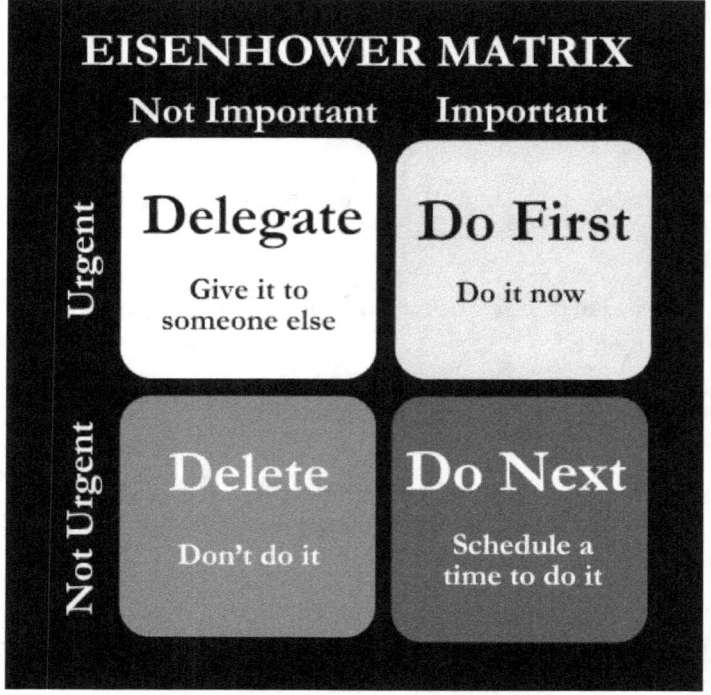

Martha stared at it like someone gazing at a mystic prophecy she could not quite read.

"So…" she murmured slowly, "I am supposed to put all my tasks into these four boxes?"

"Quadrants," Arthur corrected.

"Boxes," Martha repeated firmly.

Arthur gave up. "Yes. Boxes."

"And these boxes will tell me what to do?"

"They will tell you what to do first," Arthur clarified.

Martha frowned. "But everything needs doing first."

Arthur inhaled deeply. This, he realised, was going to be the hardest lesson yet. "Come," Arthur said. "Let us go back out into Camelot. You will choose tasks and place them in the correct 'box'."

"Quadrants," Martha muttered under her breath, imitating his tone perfectly as they left the castle.

Arthur gave her a look. "Boxes or quadrants," he conceded. "Fine."

Outside in the wonderful sunshine, the royal gardeners were arguing about carrots. Loudly.

One gardener shouted, "WE MUST PULL THEM NOW! THEY'RE READY!"

Another countered, "*No!* They need two more days at least!"

A third simply cried into a fennel bush.

Martha stepped towards them. "What seems to be the urgency?" she asked.

The head gardener pointed at the carrots dramatically. "They're at peak freshness! We risk losing the crunch!"

"Arthur," Martha whispered nervously, "is carrot crunch important?"

Arthur spoke carefully. "It depends on the context."

Martha nodded solemnly. "Right then," she said to the gardeners, "on the urgency scale, these carrots are officially... not life-threatening."

The gardeners gasped collectively.

Martha continued. "And on the importance scale, they are... not essential for the survival of Camelot."

The gardeners gasped even more loudly.

"So, these carrots," Martha declared, "for me personally, go into the not important and not urgent box. It is not a task I wish to be involved with."

One gardener fainted.

Arthur clapped politely. "Martha, that is absolutely correct. Sometimes what seems important and urgent to others is not something we need to be involved with."

She puffed up proudly. "Carrots sorted."

They walked on. They entered the main corridor and immediately collided with three groups: Knights waiting for weapons training, Maids carrying sheets for laundry duty and Villagers with baskets of grain for tax collection.

All three groups stared at Martha. "YOU TOLD *US* TO MEET YOU AT NOON!" shouted the knights.

"YOU TOLD *US* TO MEET YOU AT NOON!" shouted the maids.

"YOU TOLD *US* TO MEET YOU AT NOON!" shouted the villagers.

Martha blinked. "Oh," she whispered. "I triple-booked myself."

Arthur folded his arms. "Martha... which of these are *most* important?"

Martha pointed at the knights. "They're armed."

Arthur shook his head. "No. Think."

She pointed at the maids. "They have sheets?"

"No."

She pointed at the villagers. "They're hungry and very angry?"

Arthur nodded. "Correct."

"Because," he explained, "villagers supply the food that keeps the kingdom alive. They bring taxes which maintain the castle. They must be prioritised in this case."

Martha gasped. "Oh, my goodness. I often prioritised based on who could shout the loudest or seemed the most important!"

"Yes," Arthur said calmly. "Yes, you did."

Quickly they moved out into the bustling marketplace, where traders waved to Martha. "Martha! Did you bring the flour barrels like you promised?"

Martha froze. "I promised *what*?"

"Did you schedule the harpist for this afternoon's street performance?" another trader called.

"*What* performance?!" she said in a very surprised tone.

"And did you deliver the letter to the blacksmith?!" shouted someone else.

"*What* letter?!"

Arthur turned to her. "Martha... when did you make these promises?"

She fished out her tattered schedule, filled with doodles, arrows, correction marks, and what looked suspiciously like a drawing of Gawain wrestling a pumpkin.

"Oh... I remember now," she muttered. "These were written during my 'planning frenzy' at midnight."

Arthur nodded. "Martha, midnight is *not* planning time."

"Why not?"

"Because that's when your brain turns into soup."

Martha gasped. "It does! Midnight Soup Brain! Yes!"

Arthur continued, "You cannot commit to everything. You must learn to say 'no'."

Martha made a face as though he'd suggested eating raw onions dipped in vinegar. "I hate saying no."

"It is essential for managing time," Arthur insisted.

"No," she said stubbornly.

Arthur gave her a look.

She sighed. "OK... fine."

They made their way to the outside gates, where another group of villagers had gathered with pitchforks. "Miss Martha!" one cried. "You said you'd meet us at noon to help with the flood repairs!"

"Oh no..." Martha whispered. "I forgot about that."

"AND YOU TOLD US!" yelled another, "YOU'D BRING EXTRA CLOTHING FOR THE INJURED!"

"AND YOU PROMISED," shouted a third, "TO HELP US GATHER WOOD BEFORE THE STORM!"

Arthur looked at her with raised eyebrows. "Martha...
when were you going to do all of this?"

She opened her mouth. Closed it. Opened it again. "...I
thought I'd multitask."

Arthur pinched the bridge of his nose, partly due to the
stench coming from the villagers. "Martha... there is no
such thing. Multitasking really is a myth. You cannot do
multiple important tasks at once. None of them will ever
get done properly."

She nodded miserably. "You're right. I failed."

Arthur shook his head gently. "No, Martha. This is the
moment you learn."

He turned to the villagers. "Martha, your tasks must be
prioritised. Now put them in order." He pushed her
forward to face the group directly.

Martha stepped up, trembling slightly. "Right," she
murmured. "Let us see..."

Arthur nodded encouragingly. "Which is most urgent?"

Martha pointed to the flood victims. "They need help
now."

"Correct. And the wood gathering?"

"Urgent, but not immediately important."

"And the clothing?"

"Important, but someone else can fetch it."

Arthur beamed. "Martha... *that* is prioritisation."

She gasped. "*I did it?*!"

"Yes," he said with a broad smile.

She raised her hands triumphantly. "I am the queen of priorities!"

The villagers clapped politely.

Arthur guided Martha back towards the castle and, once inside, they entered an empty meeting room. "Martha, you must see how you spend your time. We will do a time audit."

Martha frowned. "Does that require numbers?"

"Yes."

"Oh no."

Arthur unrolled a long parchment. "We will track every minute of your time yesterday."

Martha panicked. "Oh, that was a strange day. Lots of... diversions."

Arthur cleared his throat. "Let us begin." He lifted Excalibur and the ruby pulsated a vision on the wall:

## MARTHA'S PREVIOUS DAY

**5:00am** - Attempted to wake up. Fell out of bed.

**5:10am** - Made tea. Dropped tea.

**5:30am** - Tried again. Success.

**5:40am** - Watched the sunrise "for planning inspiration".

**6:15am** - Went to market to ask for flour. Forgot to ask.

**7:00am** - Cleaned half of the kitchen.

**7:45am** - Shouted at broom, mop and bucket for being useless.

**8:00am** - Went to the gardens. Uprooted half the flowers for her ladyship.

**8:45am** - Petted the melancholy pig.

Arthur stared. "Martha... none of these were urgent or strategic."

Martha whispered, "But I was so busy."

Arthur smiled gently. "That is the danger. Feeling busy is not the same as being productive."

She gasped. "So, I have... been doing everything wrong?!"

"Not everything," Arthur said kindly. "The pig appreciated the attention."

Arthur raised his sword again. A new glowing vision appeared:

**TIME BLOCKING**

**Schedule tasks in blocks**
**Do one thing at a time**
**No distractions**
**No multitasking**

Martha stared. "This looks... organised."

"It is."

"And that is what scares me."

"It shouldn't."

Martha tilted her head. "So, I should say something like, from 9-10:00am I do XYZ. From 10-11:00am I deal with ABC. From 11:00am to noon, I fix 123."

Arthur nodded. "Yes!"

"And from 12-1:00pm... lunch?"

Arthur smiled. "Yes. You're learning."

Arthur handed Martha a clean parchment and a feather quill.

"Now," he said, "you will create a realistic schedule for tomorrow."

Martha cracked her knuckles with the confidence of a woman who had absolutely no idea what she was doing.

"Right," she said, dipping the quill into ink. "A schedule for tomorrow. Easy."

Arthur braced himself as Martha wrote:
Martha's Perfect Schedule For Tomorrow
9:00am - Everything in the kitchen that needs doing
10:00am - Everything I forgot to deal with earlier
11:00am - Fix everything that needs fixing
12:00pm - Lunch
1:00pm - Do everything again to make sure it's done

Arthur stared as though she had just written a romantic poem to a potato. "Martha," he said carefully, "this is… not a schedule."

She beamed. "Thank you!"

"That was not a compliment."

"But look!" she insisted, pointing proudly. "I have separated everything into time blocks!"

Arthur pinched the bridge of his nose. "Time blocks must contain one task. Not… all tasks known to mankind."

"Oh…" Martha said, deflating slightly.

Arthur gently pushed a fresh parchment towards her. "Try again. One task per block."

She took a breath. "Right. Yes. I can do that."

She concentrated deeply, her tongue sticking out slightly. She wrote:

7-8:00am - Help the gardeners with the vegetables
8-9:00am - Sort out the laundry
9-10:00am - Talk to the villagers about their concerns
10-11:00am - Train the cooks and maids on new recipes
11:00am-12:00pm - Prepare for lunch
12-1:00pm - Lunch is served

Arthur nodded slowly. "This… is much better."

Martha puffed up. "I am a scheduling genius!"

Arthur exhaled. "Let us not get ahead of ourselves."

The next morning at 6:45am, Arthur and Martha met beside the Round Table to implement Martha's time sheet. They left the castle and walked towards the gardens.

7-8:00am - The gardeners.

Martha rushed into the gardens ahead of Arthur, highly enthusiastic, and immediately began shouting, "RIGHT! I HAVE ONE HOUR! SHOW ME EVERYTHING YOU HAVE GOT, QUICKLY!"

The gardeners exchanged weary looks. One gardener began describing carrot progression. Another explained cabbage alignment. The third began reciting a poem about radishes.

Martha panicked. "Stop! Too many words! I only have forty-five minutes left!"

Arthur, observing from afar, sighed with ancient weariness. Coming to her side he said, "Martha... time management is about focus."

"*I am focusing!*" she barked, shaking a terrified turnip in his face. "I am focusing on *everything!*"

"No," Arthur groaned. "That is the opposite of what you should be doing."

Martha stared at the turnip. "I blame this vegetable."

8-9:00am - Sort the laundry.

At precisely 8:00am, Martha sprinted to the laundry chambers with Arthur in tow. She burst in dramatically. "RIGHT! I AM HERE TO... oh no..."

The laundry room was like a battlefield: sheets were hung from rafters like ghostly banners, towels lay in heaps, and clothes were strewn everywhere, the darning pile was the size of a horse's trough, a maid had become entangled in the sheets and was crying - someone had accidentally dyed all the King's undergarments pink.

Martha inhaled sharply. "I have fifty minutes. Let us fix this!"

Arthur was right behind her. "Martha, stop."

She froze, mid-grab of a towel.

"You cannot do all these jobs in one hour," he said quickly.

"But I have to!" she snapped back.

"Why?" he enquired.

"Because… I scheduled it!"

Arthur placed a gentle hand on her shoulder. "A schedule is not a command. It is a guide. You may adjust it. You may prioritise."

Martha blinked. "Like… rearranging things?"

"Yes."

Martha gasped softly. "Power…"

"Yes, Martha. Power."

She looked around the chaotic room. "Fine. I will just do the urgent bit. I will untangle that maid from the sheets."

Arthur nodded approvingly.

9-10:00am - Talk to the villagers.

Outside the castle gates, villagers awaited her. But not just a few. Dozens of them were waiting. Apparently, her new reputation for 'Time Mastery' had spread via excited gossip. (The villagers got the 'story' slightly wrong. Someone said Martha could 'freeze time'.)

As soon as she stepped outside, villagers surrounded her.

"Martha! Help us fix the pub roof!"

"Martha! The well is overflowing!"

"Martha! My cow will not move!"

"Martha! My husband will not move!"

She looked at Arthur helplessly. "I only have an hour!"

Arthur said, "Then prioritise."

She inhaled. "Right! Pub roof first! The well can be done second! Then the cow next! Then the husband!"

The villager with the immobile husband whispered, "That sucks."

10-11:00am - Training the cooks and maids.

Arthur guided Martha into the small training chamber. "Today," he explained, "you will teach your staff one new recipe. You have one hour."

Martha nodded. "One hour. Right." She turned to them and announced, "We are going to make... ratatouille!"

The maids groaned.

She began enthusiastically. "Right then! Ratatouille does not contain rats." She paused. "How many minutes do we have, Arthur?"

"Fifty-eight."

Martha continued. "Ratatouille contains just cut-up vegetables, that's all. Let us use this hour to learn how to cut vegetables and boil them."

The maids exchanged looks with the cooks.

Arthur raised an eyebrow. "Martha, they can do more than that. They already know how to prepare vegetables," he exhaled deeply. "This is just 'Parkinson's Law', Martha."

She blinked. "Parkinson's what?"

He pointed to the glowing sword projection:

## PARKINSON'S LAW
### Work expands to fill the time available.

Martha stared.

"So, if I have an hour, the job becomes an hour long?"

"Yes."

"But if I only gave them thirty minutes…"

Arthur nodded.

"…they could be done quicker?!" she exclaimed.

"Yes!" he said, banging his hand on his forehead.

Her jaw dropped. "I have wasted *years*."

Arthur sighed. "Yes, Martha. Yes, you probably have."

Arthur took Martha to one side. "Let us go upstairs and have a cup of tea. I do not know about you, but I am rather thirsty myself, and let us discuss how to approach the lunchtime preparation."

11:00am -12:00pm - Preparing lunch.

"Right! Now we have one hour. No chaos. No improvising. Focus, please."

Morag raised an eyebrow. "Who are you and what have you done with Martha?"

"I am prioritising," Martha declared proudly.

Morag grinned. "Well then. Let us get cooking."

Martha gave instructions, communicating clearly and concisely. She delegated and empowered, trusted them, and motivated them. The team worked efficiently, calmly, competently, for once.

Arthur looked on, proud. "This," he said softly, "is proper team time management."

And Martha whispered back, "I... like this."

After a fabulous lunch, Arthur brought Martha to the courtyard. A line of people waited for her, all loudly asking for things.

"Martha! Can you help us gather firewood?"

"Martha! Will you inspect the new potato stock?"

"Martha! Please approve my puppy for castle duty!"

"Martha! My cat will not come down from the roof!"

Martha inhaled.

Arthur whispered, "This is your final training test for today. Let us make everyone happy this time."

She lifted her chin. "I can only do *one* thing right now."

Everyone froze.

With no drama or fuss, Martha calmly and clearly said, "I will help the firewood team. The potato inspection can wait until later this afternoon. Your puppy, please bring it along tomorrow for approval, and your cat can be taken off the roof, just ask a knight to help you."

The villagers murmured. "That... makes sense."

Arthur smiled. "Martha... you've done it."

Back inside the hall, Arthur raised the sword. A glowing vision appeared:

## TIME MANAGEMENT & PRIORITISATION

Do the important things first
Ignore the unimportant things
One task per time block
No multitasking
Use schedules as guides, not orders
Use the Eisenhower Matrix
Say "no"

Martha nodded, exhausted but proud. "I think... I think I understand time now."

Arthur smiled. "No one truly understands time. But you are beginning."

She brushed hair from her face. "What's next week, Arthur?"

He shut down the vision with a flourish. "Teamwork and high-performing teams," he said.

Martha gasped. "Oh no. Not teams? The people who talk and ask questions!"

Arthur sighed. "Yes, Martha. That's them."

# CHAPTER FIVE

## Knights, Maids, And
## Why Everyone Can't Be In Charge
Teamworking

Camelot woke to the sound of arguing. Not sword fighting. Not battle training. Not the usual cursing from Tristan after he stubbed his toe on his own sword. No. This was team arguing. The worst kind. It echoed across the courtyard, down into the stables, and bounced off the castle walls like an angry flock of geese.

Martha arrived late, having already knocked over a statue, tripped over a cat, and insulted a tapestry for being hung in the wrong part of the castle. Finally, she found Arthur standing beside the Round Table, rubbing his temples with both hands.

The arguing grew louder.

"What's going on?" Martha whispered.

Arthur did not look up. "Teamwork, supposedly!"

Martha nodded sympathetically. "Oh. It sounds awful."

"It is."

"Is it contagious?" she asked with genuine intrigue.

Arthur looked at her. "No, Martha. It is not the plague."

"That's a relief. I do not know what I would do if we had one of those," she exhaled.

Just then, the doors burst open and the Knights of the Round Table surged into the hall in a chaotic knot of armour, swords, elbows, and indignation.

Gawain led the charge, waving his gauntlet angrily. "Arthur! Lancelot refuses to follow the battle plan!"

Lancelot swept in behind him, hair gleaming unnecessarily. "That is not true. I simply suggested a better plan. One with more dramatic flair, like my hair."

Bedivere stomped forward. "And I suggested it was time to listen to reason for once, but apparently logic has vacated the building."

Percival, clutching a scroll, interjected, "I created a rota. A beautifully drawn rota. No one even looked at it."

Galahad folded his arms. "I did not look at it because you used the wrong form of calligraphy on your silly rota."

Martha whispered, "Are they… always like this?"

Arthur nodded bleakly. "Every time they attempt to work together."

She nodded slowly. "I get that. My cooks start shouting whenever they're asked to share a ladle."

Arthur exhaled. "Well, today's lesson will fit perfectly, then."

The knights froze as Arthur raised a hand. "ENOUGH!" he yelled.

They stopped mid-shout, mid-gesture, mid-tantrum, and looked at Arthur.

Arthur stepped aside and gestured grandly. "Teamwork training begins now. And Martha will join us today."

Martha blinked. "What? *Why me?*"

Arthur smiled sweetly in the way that meant he was silently suffering. "Because you lead a team. And they are supposed to be a team. And both teams are… currently dysfunctional."

Martha scowled. "My team isn't dysfunctional. They just scream a lot and occasionally set cupboards on fire."

Arthur nodded sympathetically. "Yes. Precisely. Carry on as you were," he shouted to the knights. "Observe," he murmured, "this is what happens before a team becomes a team."

The knights all began speaking at once.

"I work best alone!"

"No one ever listens to me!"

"I deserve to lead this team. I have been here the longest!"

"You are incompetent and utterly useless!"

"You're barely literate. You cannot even spell your own name!"

"Your sword is compensating for something in your trousers!"

Arthur raised his sword, casting a magical crack of thunder. "STOP."

Silence.

"This," he said to Martha, "is called Storming."

Martha frowned. "Storming?"

Arthur nodded. "Yes. It is the second stage of teamwork. In the middle of the 1960s, **Bruce Tuckman** will help people understand the stages of teamwork, or so Merlin told me after one of his time travels."

He raised his sword, and a glowing image appeared in the air.

A group of stick-figure knights were arguing around a tiny Round Table. Fights were breaking out amongst them. Everyone was shouting to be heard, with no one listening at all. "Before a team performs well, they form... then they storm."

Martha gasped. "Like in my kitchen! They formed, then they stormed, then they cried, then they threatened to leave."

Arthur nodded. "That is the natural progression."

Lancelot smirked. "I do not storm. I flourish."

Bedivere groaned. "You absolutely storm. You storm so loudly people flee the room."

Arthur ignored them and walked Martha towards the castle gardens. "Come," he said softly. "You will help me demonstrate teamwork out in the garden."

As they entered the gardens, Martha blinked. Several villagers were standing around the vegetable patch, holding tools, staring at each other as though they had been forced into a group project they did not sign up for.

Arthur whispered, "These villagers have volunteered to repair the garden wall. Observe."

The villagers stared at the wall.

One pointed. "It is broken."

Another nodded. "Yes."

A third shrugged. "So, what now?"

A fourth sat down. "I am tired."

A fifth leaned on a shovel. "I am hungry."

Martha blinked. "They are rather useless," she said, shaking her head in disbelief.

Arthur shook his head. "Not entirely. They are waiting for direction. Teams do not magically organise themselves."

Martha frowned. "But I thought teamwork meant everyone does everything together at the same time."

Arthur sighed. "No, Martha. That would often be classed as a riot."

She nodded. "Oh. Yes. That makes sense. It is often a riot in the kitchen when I ask them all to clean the dirty dishes."

Arthur lifted his sword and projected another glowing illustration. On the wall, a collection of stick figures appeared representing the volunteer villagers. They stood in loose clusters, smiling awkwardly at one another. One waved. Another nodded. Several appeared to be holding different tools without knowing why.

"This," he said solemnly, "is Stage One." "It is called **Forming**," Arthur continued, "At this stage, everyone is polite. Careful. Unsure of their role. Unsure of the rules. Unsure who is actually in charge."

The figures shuffled slightly. One raised a hand, then slowly lowered it again.

"They do not yet know what they are meant to be doing," Arthur said. "So, they are very keen not to do the wrong thing."

Martha squinted at the image, then jabbed a finger at the projection. "Yes. That's like them in the kitchen. That's *exactly* them. They keep asking me what to do, then apologising while they do it."

Arthur nodded. "Forming often looks pleasant," he said. "But very little work gets done."

"Ah," Martha said. "So polite *and* useless."

Arthur chose to ignore this. With a flick of his wrist, the image dissolved, and another appeared this time the stick figures were all bumping into each other waving their tools over their heads and shouting at each other. It was a scene of total chaos and almost anarchy as they fought amongst themselves.

"And this," Arthur said, "is Stage Two. **Storming**."

Everyone in the gardens around him visibly tensed.

"At this point," Arthur explained, "people begin to understand the task, but disagree strongly about how it should be done. Roles are challenged. Authority is questioned. Frustration rises."

Martha winced. "Oh. Yes. We've been there too."

"Most teams get stuck here," Arthur said. "Because Storming feels like failure."

"Well, it certainly *feels* like it," Martha muttered. "Last Tuesday Cissy threatened to leave and become a goat herder."

Arthur inclined his head. "A classic Storming response."

The image flickered again. This time, the figures stood in a nice, neat line, and no longer at war. They passed bricks to one another. There were fewer gestures. More movement. Less noise.

"And this," Arthur said, "is Stage Three. **Norming**."

Martha leaned forward. "They look… calmer," she said.

"They are," Arthur replied. "They have begun to understand one another. Rules have emerged. Expectations are clearer. People start to trust that others will do what they said they would." "This is the stage," Arthur continued, "where productivity begins. Not because everyone agrees, but because they have learned how to disagree without everything collapsing, including the wall!"

Martha folded her arms slowly. "So Forming is awkward politeness," she said. "Storming is chaos and emotional outbursts. And Norming is when people finally stop shouting and get on with it."

Arthur nodded proudly. "Exactly."

He flicked the ruby in the sword once more. "And this," he said, revealing the final glowing scene, "is **Performing**."

The stick figures had built the wall so efficiently, they were moving onto their next task, making a gate and preparing a vegetable patch and one person had time to drink tea."

Martha pointed. "That one's me."

Arthur arched an eyebrow. "I would expect you to choose the one drinking tea."

She shrugged. "A leader must maintain hydration."

Arthur turned to the villagers and said to Martha, "Right. Let us move them out of Forming into Storming, onto Norming, and finally Performing."

"Do we have to go through Storming?" Martha asked.

"Yes."

"Can we not skip it?"

"No."

"Why not?" she said, with pleading eyes.

"It is where the shouting happens and the fun begins," he said, with a naughty-boy grin.

"Oh! That is *so* not necessary," she said, with a huge sigh.

"Yes, it is," said Arthur firmly, still grinning like a Cheshire cat.

The villagers began arguing about who should carry the stones.

"We are into the Storming," Arthur murmured.

One villager shouted, "I carried the stones last time!"

Another yelled, "You carried one stone!"

A third shouted, "We should use smaller stones!"

A fourth yelled, "Use bigger stones to get it done quicker!"

A fifth yelled, "Let us go home!"

Martha folded her arms. "I hate this part."

Arthur nodded. "So does every leader."

She sighed. "Fine. What now?"

Arthur gestured towards the villagers. "You have to guide them through and out of the Storming stage, into the Norming stage."

Martha inhaled. "Quiet!" she shouted. "No one is going home. We are fixing this wall."

Arthur winced. "Martha, a little less aggressive. We do not want to exasperate the storm."

She moderated. "Right... sorry. Let us try again. Villagers! We need your help to fix the wall. So let us all get organised."

A villager raised a hand. "Who's in charge?"

Martha froze. "Um... that would be me?" She looked towards Arthur for approval.

Arthur nodded approvingly, as she expected, although she wished he had not.

Another villager asked, "What do we do first?"

Martha looked helplessly at Arthur.

He whispered, "Roles. Give them roles to do."

Martha puffed up proudly. She knew all about rolls. "You, you are on cheese and onion. And you, ham and tomato. And you, tuna and sweetcorn, with mayonnaise."

Arthur held up his hand. "STOP!" he shouted. "Martha, I was talking 'roles'." He spelled it out slowly. "r-o-l-e-s. And not," he continued, "r-o-l-l-s for eating."

Martha looked at him, then at the villagers. "You can make those rolls later," she said, "but for now I need...*You*, to gather stones. *You*, to stack them. *You*, to mix the mud. You, to pass the stones. *You*, to stop complaining you're hungry now, from all the talk of rolls, and help out."

The villagers blinked and started to move about slowly.

The complaining villager muttered, "That feels targeted. You started the roll talk."

But they were moving. Slowly. Disjointedly. Then more smoothly. Then with purpose.

Martha gasped. "It is working!"

Arthur nodded warmly. "Norming," he said, with a twinkle in his eye.

Within minutes, the villagers formed a neat line, passing stones, patting mud, stacking bricks.

Martha clapped excitedly. "They're doing it! They're a team!"

Arthur smiled proudly. "This is now Performing."

One villager shouted, "MARTHA! THE WALL IS HALFWAY DONE!"

Another shouted, "AND NO ONE HAS ARGUED FOR FIVE MINUTES!"

A third shouted, "I HAVE NOT SAT DOWN ONCE!"

Martha beamed. "This feels… wonderful."

Arthur nodded. "Yes. That is teamwork."

Martha whispered, "My kitchen could be like this."

Arthur hesitated, but said gently, "In theory, yes, it could."

Martha's eyes glowed with hope. "In practice?" she asked.

Arthur coughed. "We will... discuss that later."

The villagers finished rebuilding the garden wall, cheering and hugging.

Martha stared, amazed. "I did that...?"

Arthur shook his head kindly. "No, Martha. They did that. You simply gave the instructions."

Martha blushed. "Oh. That's... nice. Shall we make the rolls now? I fancy a tuna and sweetcorn."

Arthur shook his head and gestured for her to follow him to the courtyard, where the knights were still bickering loudly around the Round Table inside the chamber.

She groaned. "Are you going to fix them, or do I need to do it?"

Arthur smiled. "You have the skill to do it now, Martha."

Martha sighed deeply. "Right. Fine. Let us fix the disasters that are wearing the armour."

Arthur clapped his hands. "Now you are thinking like a leader."

Martha followed Arthur into the chamber and to the Round Table, where the knights had already resumed arguing. Gawain was pacing in furious circles. Bedivere looked ready to throw a scroll. Percival had retreated to a corner to weep quietly over his rota. Lancelot checked his hair in his shield.

"Perfect," Arthur muttered. "All the dysfunction we could possibly need."

Martha sighed. "It is like watching my maids fight over a duster."

Arthur raised Excalibur, and the tip glowed a soft pink. "Martha," he said, "next we will learn about the work of another future scholar, a wise man who understood that every team needs different roles. That's *r-o-l-e-s*, not *r-o-l-l-s*. His name is…" he paused dramatically, "…**Dr. Meredith Belbin**."

The sword projected nine glowing pictures above the table: a rose, an explorer, a chair, a triangle, Le Penseur, an ant, a tractor, an alarm clock, and a hedgehog - each representing a team role. As Arthur went on to point out, Dr. Belbin would probably come up with better names in years to come.

Martha squinted. "Why is one of them a hedgehog?"

"That is a depiction of the 'Specialist', Martha."

"Oh. Well, it looks prickly."

"They usually are," Arthur said, and gestured towards his knights. "To understand Belbin's team roles, we shall demonstrate them using your favourite subjects."

"The maids?" Martha asked hopefully.

"No, Martha. The knights."

She groaned. "Fine."

Arthur pointed to each picture from the projection in turn and showcased to Martha each of the knights he believed fitted each role, without them knowing.

**A Rose - *Creates***

Strength: Ideas, imagination, creativity.

Weakness: Easily distracted, impractical, head in the clouds.

Arthur gestured towards Galahad, who stood staring at the ceiling, muttering something about designing a collapsing drawbridge that fell upward.

Martha frowned. "He's thinking about nonsense again."

"Creative solutions," Arthur corrected.

"That's nonsense."

Arthur sighed. "Yes. But it is creative nonsense."

## An Explorer - *Investigates*

Strength: Enthusiastic, good at connecting with others, enjoys research.

Weakness: Loses interest, easily distracted, tends to work alone.

Arthur pointed at Lancelot, who was currently examining the tapestry.

Martha blinked. "He's hitting on the carpet."

"It is called a tapestry."

"He's hitting on the tapestry-carpet that's on the wall. Why?"

Lancelot heard them and winked. "A gentleman explores all... possibilities, both past and present."

Arthur inhaled through clenched teeth.

## A Chair - *Co-ordinates*

Strength: Organises, delegates, clarifies roles and responsibilities.

Weakness: Might offload responsibility, become dictatorial, closed to other suggestions.

Arthur gestured at Percival, who stood clutching his beloved rota with trembling reverence.

Percival cleared his throat. "If everyone would just follow the system, we would be fine!"

Martha nodded. "He loves his charts, does Percival."

"Yes," Arthur said. "That is his entire personality."

## A Triangle - *Shapes*

Strength: Moves in the right direction, pushes progress, challenges ineffectiveness.

Weakness: Aggressive, impatient, plays devil's advocate for the sake of it.

Arthur indicated Gawain, who immediately shouted, "I AM NOT IMPATIENT! MOVE ASIDE SO I CAN EXPLAIN WHY YOU ARE WRONG!"

Martha winced. "He's frightening, though. He makes the maids anxious."

"Yes," Arthur said. "That is a typical triangle who likes to be the shaper of the team."

## Le Penseur - *Evaluates*

Strength: Logical, strategic, analyses problems and data, balanced.

Weakness: Overly critical, slow to decide, can hold back progress.

Arthur pointed towards Bedivere, who was analysing the layout of the Round Table.

"Well," Bedivere muttered to himself, "if we shifted this table three degrees clockwise, the acoustics would improve. But then again, perhaps no. Wait. Perhaps... hmm. No."

Martha whispered, "He's still deciding."

Arthur nodded. "He actually began that thought last Tuesday afternoon."

## An Ant -*Teams*

Strength: Diplomacy, harmony, supportive, teamwork.

Weakness: Indecisive, avoids conflict, often overlooked or not seen.

Arthur pointed to Tristan; a knight so inoffensively pleasant that most people forgot he was in the room until he offered them tea.

Tristan stepped forward. "I think... um... perhaps... if it is all right... we could... not fight?"

Gawain glared.

Tristan immediately backed away. "I am sorry, Gawain. I am only trying to help everyone out!"

Arthur nodded gently. "That is a real team worker, smoothing everything and everyone out."

## A Tractor - *Implements*

Strength: Practical, reliable, committed, self-disciplined, systematic.

Weakness: Resistant to change, forgets the bigger picture, is led rather than leads.

Arthur gestured at Ector. "He is still using a broom from fifteen years ago and refusing to consider replacing it."

"If it was good enough then," Ector grumbled, "it is good enough now."

Martha muttered, "He reminds me of an old kitchen mop that refuses to die."

## An Alarm Clock - *Completes*

Strength: Detail, accuracy, works to timescale, sense of urgency.

Weakness: Anxiety, overwork, preoccupied, lacks ideas.

Arthur nodded towards Lionel, who was polishing his sword so aggressively that sparks were flying.

"I just want it finished off perfectly!" Lionel cried, weeping openly.

Martha nodded empathetically. "He needs a lie down before he bursts a blood vessel."

## A Hedgehog - *Specialist*

Strength: Knowledgeable, methodical, factual.

Weakness: Narrow focus, prickly, isolated.

Arthur pointed at Merlin, who was not actually a knight, but had inserted himself into the circle anyway.

"I know one million spells!" Merlin boasted.

Tristan whispered back, "You only know two."

Merlin hissed, "But they are very complicated spells."

Arthur lowered his sword, and the pictures vanished before them. "Those," he said, "were Belbin's team roles. Every team needs a balance of them."

Martha nodded slowly. "But my team only has Morag, Cissy, and a few others."

Arthur smiled. "Then we will find out their roles today."

Martha gasped. "Do I get to tell them?"

"No," Arthur said quickly. "Absolutely not." Arthur clapped his hands sharply. "Right! Knights, come round!" He then yelled down the staircase to Martha's maids and cooks, "WOULD YOU ALL PLEASE COME UPSTAIRS NOW? OUR TEAMWORK TRAINING TEST BEGINS NOW!"

He produced two scrolls. "One for each team."

Martha squinted. "What's on the scroll?"

Arthur smiled. "A list of ten items hidden around Camelot. You must find them all, together, in your teams."

Gawain puffed out his chest. "A competition?"

Arthur nodded. "Yes."

Lancelot adjusted his hair. "Victory shall be mine!"

Percival held up his rota. "I have a structure ready!"

Bedivere muttered, "The logic of a scavenger hunt is flawed…"

Before Arthur could continue, Martha grabbed her scroll from Arthur's hand. "What do we need to find?" she asked. She unfolded her list and looked long and hard at it.

THE GREAT CAMELOT SCAVENGER HUNT

1. A golden apple
2. The Queen's missing glove
3. A glowing pebble
4. A frog wearing a ribbon
5. A spoon with a bite taken out of it

6. A lost helmet
7. A red feather
8. The jester's left shoe
9. The smallest vegetable in the gardens
10. A blue scroll hidden somewhere in the castle

Martha blinked. "What on earth is that list?!"

Arthur smiled serenely. "A test."

Gawain shouted, "KNIGHTS, ASSEMBLE IN THE COURTYARD!"

They trampled out of the room chaotically.

Martha whispered to Arthur, "Should we let them run? They look like a stampede."

Arthur shrugged. "That is their process."

Martha frowned at her team. Cissy was already overwhelmed. Morag already annoyed. Eve already lost and as for Alice... well. Martha exhaled loudly. "All right, everyone. Let us become a team."

Morag cracked her neck. "Right. Who does what?"

Martha held up the scroll. This was her moment. Belbin... would guide them.

"Oh!" she gasped suddenly. "I get it!"

Arthur raised an eyebrow. "You... get it?"

"Yes! Belbin's roles!"

Morag frowned. "Who's Belbin? Is he the new stable boy?"

Martha ignored her. "Cissy, you're an Ant! You help everyone else and keep harmony."

Cissy beamed. "I like harmony!"

"Morag, you're the Triangle. You push us forward, but you're always impatient."

Morag grinned. "Oh, I am better than a circle. I have three sharp points."

"Eve, you…um…are the tractor. Just do things. Safely."

Eve saluted.

"And me?" Martha asked Arthur rather loudly.

Arthur answered kindly, "You are the Chair. You organise. You bring people together. You see the whole picture. Which is fitting, as you always used to sit in one all day long."

Martha blinked. "But… I like sitting down."

Arthur smiled. "Yes. But today… you will stand and lead."

Martha inhaled deeply. "Right. Team! Let us find these stupid items."

And so, it began.

## Item 1: The Golden Apple

Morag sprinted straight to the orchard. Cissy followed, shouting, "DON'T RUN SO FAST!" Eve ran into a tree, and Alice followed into her.

Martha sighed.

Arthur murmured, "Storming begins…"

## Item 2: The Queen's Missing Glove

The glove was rumoured to be somewhere near Guinevere's chambers.

Martha whispered, "Cissy… diplomacy."

Cissy knocked timidly.

Guinevere opened the door. "What do you want now?"

Cissy squeaked, "Glove?"

Guinevere glared at her, with a hard stare and pursed lips.

Cissy fainted.

Morag shoved past Martha. "I will handle this."

She stomped into the Queen's room and began searching aggressively under cushions.

Guinevere shrieked, "GET OUT!"

Morag muttered, "Storming indeed."

## Item 3: A Glowing Pebble

Eve spotted one immediately. "LOOK!" she shouted, picking up a pebble. It did not glow. She shook it violently. Still no glow. She frowned. "I will chew it. That might make it glow."

Martha yanked it away before Eve could swallow it.

Meanwhile, the knights had been getting themselves ready, slowly but surely. Arthur watched them through a magical projection. They argued continuously.

"No, you take the pebble!"

"No, you!"

"Where's Lionel?"

"He wandered off polishing something!"

"Who ate the spoon?!"

Arthur shook his head.

"Belbin imbalance," he murmured. "Too many Triangles. Not enough Ants."

## Item 4: A Frog Wearing a Ribbon

Cissy spotted the frog. Morag caught it. Alice tied the ribbon on the wrong frog. The frog attacked her. More chaos continued.

## Items 5–10

Martha's team:
- Found the bitten spoon (thanks to Morag smashing open a drawer)
- Found the helmet (by accident, it fell on Eve's head)
- Found the red feather (Martha bribed a red bird with breadcrumbs and pulled one out)
- Found the jester's left shoe (in the moat, Alice fell in retrieving it)
- Found the smallest vegetable (Cissy held up a pea triumphantly)
- Finally found the blue scroll (Morag spotted it behind a tapestry)

They returned to Arthur in the courtyard: soaked, bruised, covered in mud, proud, exhausted, but… a team.

The knights returned thirty minutes later, having found only the shoe.

Gawain cried, "Lionel, it is the wrong shoe, that's the right shoe!"

Lionel cried, "How can it be the wrong shoe if it is the right shoe?!"

Gawain tried again. "It is the right shoe, but it is the wrong shoe!"

Bedivere intervened, "Lionel, we needed the left shoe, not the right shoe!"

Arthur, shaking his head at the stupidity of the shoes, turned to Martha. "Well?"

She puffed her chest. "We are a *team*."

Arthur nodded warmly. "Yes. Yes, you are."

The knights slumped down onto the courtyard floor: armour dented, hair frazzled, one missing a boot, another missing a sense of dignity. Lionel sobbed quietly into the shoe that was not left, but was not right for the hunt.

Arthur surveyed them with the expression of a schoolteacher finding his class sniffing cow-gum glue. "You found one item," he said gently, "and even that was not the right item."

"We found more," Gawain snapped. "We simply lost them again."

Bedivere sighed. "And in my case, I lost interest when we did not know our left from right."

Percival held up his rota. "My schedule was *perfect*. But no one *followed* it."

Tristan smiled apologetically. "I did make tea for everyone."

Lancelot flicked his hair. "I provided morale and knowledge of how others can do this."

Arthur closed his eyes. "Martha," he said, "I think it is time you explained what went wrong."

Martha blinked. "Me?"

Arthur nodded. "Yes. You understand this lesson. Teach them."

Martha had never been asked to teach knights before. Normally she was asked to stop shouting at them. This was different. This was… leadership. She stepped forward, trembling slightly, then straightened her apron with authority. "Right then, you lot," she said. "You are terrible at being a team, because you're all acting the same, although you could all be very different if you listened to each other's strengths."

Gawain bristled. "We are absolutely not the same!"

"You are *all* acting like Triangles," Martha said bluntly. "And you storm everywhere you go like angry weather."

Bedivere raised a hand. "I am Le Penseur."

"No," Martha corrected. "You *think* you are. But most of the time you're just judging things and never deciding what to actually do."

Bedivere looked crushed. "That is… extremely fair."

Percival frowned. "Then what about me?"

"You," Martha said gently, "are a Chair… in theory. But you don't sit and work it through, you just issue lots of schedules that no one actually reads."

Percival gasped, clutching his rota. "That is my whole identity!"

Lancelot smirked. "And what am I?"

"An Explorer," Martha said. "You talk to everyone, find things out. Which is useful, if you could stop flirting with half the kingdom whilst doing it."

A passing maid giggled, and Lancelot winked reflexively.

"SEE?!" Martha yelled.

Tristan sipped his tea. "What about me?"

"You're the Ant," Martha said. "The one who tries hard to work at the task in hand. The harmony when things get distracted. The only one preventing mass combat in corridors, with a cup of tea."

Tristan smiled modestly and offered her an Earl Grey.

Arthur watched proudly. She was teaching. And they were listening.

Martha turned to Arthur. "Some teams aren't balanced because no one has ever told them that they *need* balance."

Arthur nodded. "Correct."

The knights shifted awkwardly.

"So," Martha announced, "we're going to *rebalance* the team. Belbin style. Camelot edition."

Arthur projected the nine Belbin roles again.

Martha walked among the knights like a talent scout forced to pick from a group of overgrown, armoured toddlers. "We know that Lancelot likes to be an Explorer, so he will remain in that role," she said, looking him up and down with a look of disdain. "Next, we need a Rose. Someone creative. Someone who thinks differently. Someone…"

"Galahad," Arthur whispered.

"Yes! Him! Galahad, you are perfect!"

Galahad blinked. "I thought I was already doing that?"

"You were," Martha said. "You just did not know why."

Galahad smiled proudly. "So, my strange ideas… are useful?"

Martha nodded. "Sometimes. Not always."

He beamed.

"Next, we need that tractor."

No knight moved. All looked allergic to doing.

Finally, Ector raised a tentative hand. "I… suppose… I am a reliable tractor. I keep going the same way without breaking down."

"Yes," Martha said. "And as stubborn as slow tractors on the road when you want to get past them. You will be perfect."

Ector nodded happily.

"Now, we need an Alarm Clock." She looked around at the others.

Lionel stepped forward, eyes wide, polishing cloth in hand. "That will be me."

"Yes," Martha said carefully. "But please stop crying on the weapons."

He sniffed loudly. "I will try…"

"Now for a Hedgehog."

Merlin shouted from behind a hedge, "IT IS ME! I AM SPECIAL!"

Arthur sighed. "Yes, Merlin, that you are. Very special."

"And we need a real Chair." Martha pointed to Percival. "*You*. But you must stop scheduling and sitting on people's emotions."

Percival nodded earnestly. "But can I still colour-code them?"

"No," Martha replied. "And now, we need a proper Triangle."

Three knights stepped forward, and then Gawain stepped forward once more.

"Oh good," Martha added. "Gawain will do fine. We do not need more."

The two other knights stepped back sadly.

"And the Le Penseur is you…" Martha said, turning to Bedivere. "Try deciding *one* thing today. Just start with one thing."

Bedivere inhaled with heroic resolve. "I shall attempt… a decision."

Arthur whispered, "This is the bravest thing I have ever seen."

"And of course Tristan," Martha continued, "we always need you as our Ant."

Tristan raised his teacup. "I brought biscuits, as well as a special treat."

"Perfect," Martha said. "You're hired."

The knights now stood in a balanced formation. It was chaotic. Uncomfortable. And strange. But it was balance.

Arthur looked moved. "Martha… you've done it."

"I have?" she whispered.

"Yes," he said, with a warm smile on his face.

She inhaled deeply. "So, we test them again?"

Arthur grinned. "Yes. Another teamwork challenge."

The knights all groaned.

Arthur placed a small, locked chest in the middle of the courtyard. "Inside this chest," he said, "is your next quest."

The knights leaned in, excitedly.

"You may not open the chest until you solve the riddle... together." He handed the riddle to Martha.

Martha read it aloud: "I belong to all and am used by all; I am everything and nothing at once. Seek me not with your eyes, but with order, for chaos becomes me when I am ignored."

The knights stared blankly.

Gawain shrugged. "Is it... me?"

"No," Martha groaned.

Lancelot smoothed his hair. "Is it... charm?"

"No."

Bedivere began listing possibilities mathematically. Percival tried to schedule possible answers. Lionel panicked. Tristan offered tea. Ector tried to hit the chest with a broom.

Arthur sighed. "Martha, guide them. Use Belbin."

She inhaled. "Right. Rose goes first."

Galahad stepped forward, his eyes gleaming. "It is time," he announced dramatically. "It must be time. You cannot see it, but we all use it."

Martha's jaw dropped. "That's… correct."

Gawain looked offended. "He guessed!"

Arthur cleared his throat. "Good teams allow the Rose to dream first."

The chest clicked open. Inside was another scroll. Arthur gestured. "Open it."

Martha unrolled it.

The Final Team Task
- Build a bridge across the courtyard using only the materials provided.
- You have one hour.
- You must all contribute.
- No shouting.

The knights exchanged uneasy looks.

"AN HOUR?" Lionel screeched.

"No shouting?" Gawain repeated nervously.

"I must contribute?" Lancelot muttered.

Arthur whispered to Martha, "High-performing teams combine all roles."

Martha nodded.

"Right team!" she barked, then softened. "Sorry. Right… team. Let us Belbin this bridge."

And they did. Kind of.

**Galahad (Rose)** invented a new type of bridge shaped like an upside-down teacup. It was terrible. But imaginative.

**Percival (Chair)** organised tasks, delegated fairly, and made a rota no one read, but everyone vaguely followed.

**Gawain (Triangle)** motivated everyone by shouting less loudly than usual. For him, a miracle, and he often questioned "Why?" they were doing the task.

**Bedivere (Le Penseur)** actually decided: "We will *not* use wet hay as a structural element." Everyone applauded.

**Ector (Tractor)** built the base. Efficiently. No nonsense.

**Lionel (Alarm Clock)** smoothed every plank, polished every nail, and panicked only three times that they might run out of time.

**Tristan (Ant)** stopped two fights, handed out tea and biscuits, and told everyone they were doing wonderfully. He might be the reason they finished at all.

**Lancelot (Explorer)** procured rope, nails, and a hammer from the villagers and at least two admirers. All useful, apart from the admirers.

**Merlin (Hedgehog)** cast exactly one spell. It made the wood smell like lavender. Morale improved.

And under Martha's careful, surprisingly patient eye, the bridge... stood. Crooked slightly. Leaning to the left. Probably illegal under modern building regulations. But it stood. And everyone had built it. Together.

The knights erupted into cheers.

Arthur folded his arms proudly. "Martha... this is high performance."

She glowed. "My first high-performing team..."

Arthur nodded. "Yes."

She gasped. "I want to frame it!"

"No."

"Just a small painting then, maybe!"

"No."

"Fine. It will remain in my memory," she said, rather annoyed.

Back at the Round Table, Arthur projected the final message of the day.

## TEAMWORK & HIGH PERFORMING TEAMS

**Teams need balance**
**Roles have strengths and weaknesses**
**Storming is natural**
**Coordination matters**
**Everyone contributes**
**No one role wins**
**Collaboration beats heroics**

Martha nodded slowly. "This… was my favourite so far."

Arthur smiled warmly. "I thought it might be."

She then gasped. "Oh no, Arthur. What are we learning next week?"

Arthur straightened. "Problem Solving & Decision-Making."

Martha's face fell. "Oh dear. I hate problems."

Arthur chuckled. "Then it will be a big day next week."

She groaned.

"But don't worry," Arthur added gently. "There will be plenty of decisions to practise."

Martha whispered, "That's the part I hate most."

Arthur sighed. "Yes. I know.

# CHAPTER SIX

## Hats, Problems, And
## Thinking Sideways On Purpose
Problem Solving & Decision Making

The trouble began before sunrise.

Arthur knew it would be a long day the moment he heard a distant BOOM, followed by Eve yelling, "I DID NOT MEAN TO!"

...and then Alice shouting, "SEE, IT WASN'T ME!"

Arthur closed his eyes. Not again.

He hurried towards the kitchens and found the corridor filled with smoke, feathers, flour, and something that might once have been soup, but had now reached a consistency known only in nightmares, spread across the floor. Martha stumbled out of the haze, coughing, covered in soot.

Arthur's eyes widened. "Martha! What happened?"

She threw her hands up in despair. "*I don't know!* There was a noise! Then a smell! A *thing* exploded! Eve panicked! Alice screamed! I screamed! Then *something* caught fire! Then *everything* caught fire! Then *something else* caught fire! Then I lost track of it all!"

Arthur peered past her. Eve was attempting to sweep smoke away with a broom, ineffectively. Alice was trying to calm a goose who had somehow acquired singed eyebrows.

He sighed deeply. "Martha... this looks like a problem."

"*Yes!*" she cried. "*A very big one!*"

Arthur gave her a gentle but knowing look. "And today... we will learn how to solve problems."

Martha froze. "Oh no," she said, turning away.

"Yes."

"Well, can we not start tomorrow?" she pleaded.

"No."

"Next week then?"

"No."

"In the next lifetime, perhaps?"

"No."

Martha groaned. This battle, she was going to lose.

Problem solved.

Once the smoke in the kitchen settled, thanks largely to Eve, who accidentally knocked the window open with her head, Arthur surveyed the mess. A massive cauldron sat on the floor with a huge crack down the side. The firepit stones had exploded outward across the entire floor. Flour dust coated everything, and half a dozen eggs had been fried in mid-air and were now precariously stuck to the ceiling, next to a spoon that was also embedded up there. Finally, as he surveyed the room, Arthur could see a very offended goose, honking at everyone while standing in what looked suspiciously like pink custard.

Arthur took a slow breath. "Martha. What *exactly* triggered this disaster?"

Martha looked at Eve. Eve looked at Alice. Alice pointed at the goose. The goose honked the kind of honk that said, do not blame me.

Martha shrugged helplessly. "We do not know."

Arthur nodded. "So, this," he said calmly, "is the real problem, not knowing! Not the explosion. Not the broken cauldron. Not the goose." The goose honked indignantly again. Arthur continued, "The real problem is that we don't know the cause of the incident."

Martha gasped. "So, we must do more problems to find out?!"

"No, Martha," Arthur said patiently. "We must find the root cause."

Arthur lifted his sword. A glowing image formed in the air, of a tree, its roots spreading deep into the ground.

"We begin problem solving," he said, "by digging beneath the symptoms, to find the underlying cause."

Martha squinted. "So… it is like digging for carrots, or turnips, or potatoes?"

"Yes," Arthur said slowly. "But with fewer vegetables."

The glowing tree illustration labelled itself:

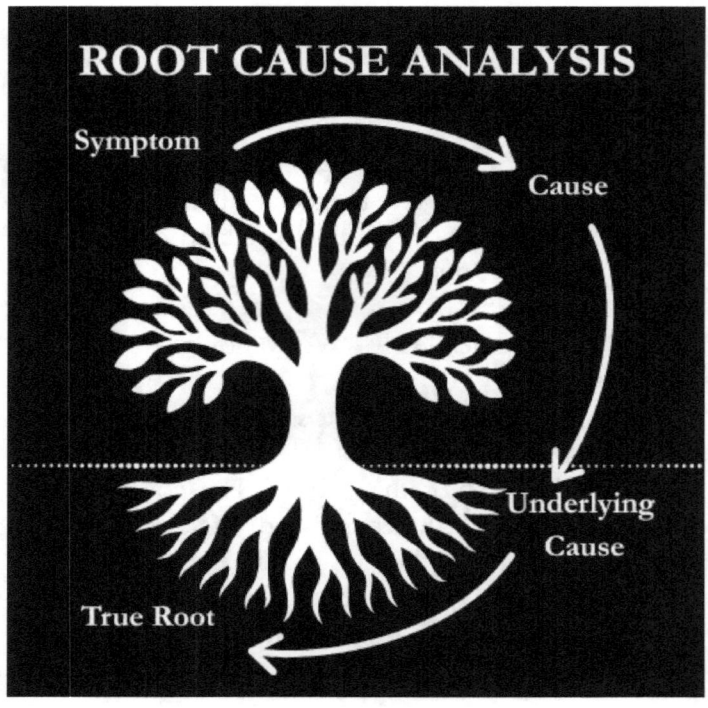

Eve raised her hand timidly. "Is the root cause sometimes me?"

The whole kitchen nodded immediately, and echoes of "Yes." were heard around the room.

Arthur cleared his throat diplomatically. "Let us assume the cause is… not Eve for now."

Eve looked relieved. Alice raised her hand. "Is it sometimes me?"

Martha and Eve responded in unison. "Yes."

Arthur moved on quickly. "Martha," he said, "let us walk backwards from the disaster." He pointed at the cracked cauldron. "*What* caused the cauldron to crack and explode?"

Martha frowned. "Well… it overheated."

"Good. And *what* caused it to overheat?"

Alice raised her hand. "We added too much wood to the fire."

Eve added, "…Way too much wood to the fire."

"And *what* caused that?"

Martha thought. "Oh! Because Morag said we needed the stew cooked faster!"

Arthur nodded. "And *what* caused that?"

Silence. Until Cissy whispered, "Because Martha told us lunch had to be done by 10:00am, even though lunch is at noon."

Arthur turned to Martha slowly. "Martha... why?"

"I was trying out my time management!" she wailed.

Arthur exhaled. "And who told you to speed up lunch?"

Martha blinked. "Oh! Guinevere did! She said she needed lunch early for a surprise meeting that her maid had told her about, but I thought that was tomorrow."

Arthur nodded. "Aha!" He traced the root cause chain across the ceiling as it had been described: "The cauldron cracked and exploded *because*: the fire was too hot *because*, Eve and Alice overshot the instructions *because*, Morag was under pressure for speed *because*, Martha issued an unrealistic deadline *because*, Guinevere wrongly believed she needed lunch early *because*, her maid had misread her calendar."

Martha gasped. "It wasn't the explosion that was the problem. It was the... maid's calendar?!"

Arthur smiled. "And that, Martha, is root cause analysis."

Martha slapped her forehead. "I cannot believe the problem wasn't the goose."

The goose honked smugly.

Arthur gestured. "Martha... now we can solve problems using another tool. A tool involving hats."

Martha straightened. "I *love* hats, especially at weddings."

"That enthusiasm worries me," Arthur muttered.

He waved his sword again. Six colours projected above them:

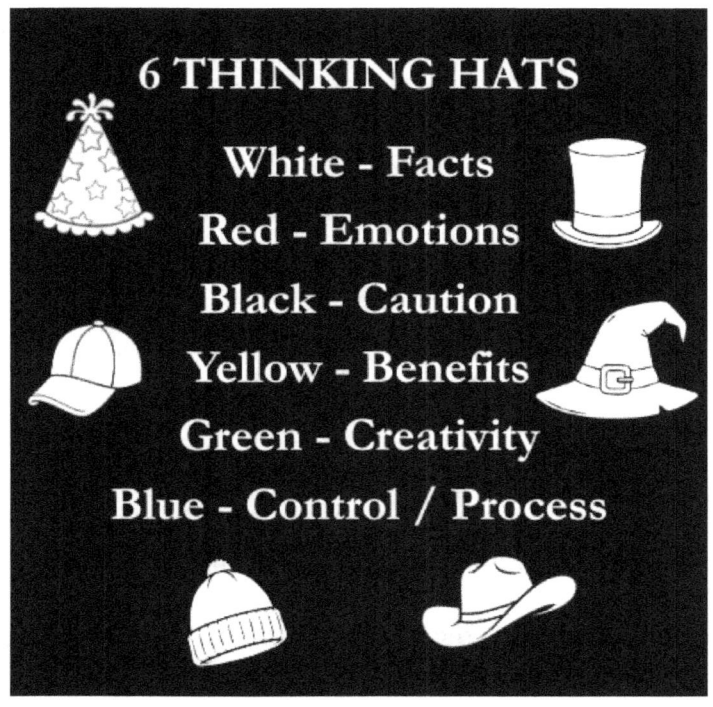

"We will think through each hat, just as **Edward de Bono** will describe in 1985," Arthur said.

But Martha wasn't listening. She was already yanking tablecloths, bowls, ribbons, vegetables, fabric scraps, and three entire curtains to begin crafting hats.

Eve pointed nervously. "Should she... should she be doing that?"

"No," Arthur whispered. "But we're committed now."

In ten minutes, Martha had produced the 6 most hideous hats Camelot had ever seen.

**White Hat**: A huge turnip strapped to a bonnet with string. "Facts are crunchy," Martha explained.

**Red Hat**: A bright red feathered monstrosity that made the goose honk in offence.

**Black Hat**: A burnt old pot with holes in it. "To represent pessimism," Martha clarified.

**Yellow Hat**: A hat made of buttercups and actual butter. It started to melt instantly.

**Green Hat**: A vegetable crown of sprouting bits of spinach and broccoli.

**Blue Hat:** A large blue mixing bowl turned upside down.

Arthur stared at the pile of horrors. "Right..." he murmured faintly. "Let us... begin."

Martha clapped. "Team! We will fix our exploding cauldron problem using the hats!"

Eve whispered, "I think the problem is the hats."

Arthur shushed her.

## White Hat - *Facts Only*

Martha sat at the table and put on the turnip helmet. "*Facts!*" she declared. The turnip wobbled dangerously. "We know the cauldron exploded because the fire was too hot. Morag insisted we speed everything up because I rushed her, but it was Guinevere who started the chaos because her maid had misread the calendar."

Arthur nodded. "Good. No emotions."

The turnip fell into Martha's lap. She took a bite, then ignored it.

## Red Hat - *Feelings*

Cissy placed the feathered red hat on her head and burst into tears immediately. "I feel scared!" she wailed. "And guilty! And hot in this hat!"

Arthur nodded sympathetically. "Good. We express emotions so they don't cloud the next steps."

The goose stole the red hat and ran away. No one stopped it.

## Black Hat - *Caution*

Morag donned the burnt pot. "This was a stupid idea," she said immediately. "We're all being idiots. This is hopeless. Nothing will be solved this way."

Arthur nodded. "Yes. That is the Black Hat."

Morag looked pleased.

## Yellow Hat - *Optimism*

Alice placed the buttercup and butter hat on her head. It continued to melt all over her face. "This feels... positive?" she said cheerfully.

"Why?" Arthur asked.

"Because it smells like pancakes, and I love pancakes!" she said with a dreamy smile on her face.

Arthur blinked. "Well... that is misguided optimism, I suppose."

## Green Hat - *Creativity*

Eve wore the spinach and broccoli crown. "I have an idea!" she shouted.

Everyone ducked.

Eve continued, "What if we build a special cauldron that *cannot* explode?"

Arthur considered. "That is actually... a useful idea."

Eve smiled proudly.

## Blue Hat - *Control/Process*

Arthur placed the large blue mixing bowl on his own head. He regretted it instantly. "Right," he said from under the bowl, "we have the facts, the feelings, the risks, the benefits, and the ideas. Now we must decide."

## Decision-Making Time

Arthur helped Martha document options using the pink illumination from his sword like a pen. After several debates, shouting incidents, and another small fire (Eve), they concluded: They needed a sturdier cauldron. A clearer chain of communication. A realistic timeframe. A daily calendar check. And no more "lunch at 10:00am" unless it was brunch.

Martha nodded proudly. She had invented the concept of brunch, which she said would catch on one day. Everyone would call it Martha's Brunch, and a chain of restaurants would pop up everywhere offering it. "Yes. Yes. *Yes*! This is problem solving!" she declared enthusiastically.

Arthur exhaled. "Yes, Martha. For the first time… it is."

Arthur gestured. "And now, Martha, you will run a brainstorming session, which in years to come will be known as board storming, to prevent future crises."

Martha gasped. *"Me? In charge?"*

"Yes," he said with an encouraging look.

She puffed up confidently. "Right then! Everyone gather round! We are going to brainstorm some solutions to our problem!"

Arthur braced himself.

Martha clapped. "RULES!" she shouted. "Rule number one: No shouting!"

Arthur winced.

"Rule number two: No bad ideas!"

Eve raised her hand. "What if we outlaw fire completely?"

"*No*, now that's not a real answer, is it!"

Arthur whispered, "During brainstorming, you don't say no, or criticise someone's ideas."

Martha glared. "But that idea was terrible."

"The point," Arthur said, "is that *any* idea may spark a *good* idea. It is called cross-fertilisation."

Martha sighed. "Fine. Eve, thank you for your… fireless Camelot idea."

Eve saluted proudly.

Alice raised her hand. "What if we use two cauldrons, so if one explodes, the other is fine?"

Arthur blinked. "…Better than expected."

Morag raised a hand. "What if we have a rotating stew duty, so no one gets overwhelmed?"

Arthur smiled warmly. "Excellent."

Cissy sniffled. "What if we label the maid's calendar properly?"

"Yes!" Arthur said. "Very good."

The brainstorm continued until Martha gasped dramatically. "We've done it! We solved problems! We made decisions!"

Arthur nodded. "And we will refine them further tomorrow."

Martha frowned. "Tomorrow?"

Arthur smiled. "Yes. Because we still have much more to try out and learn."

\*\*\*\*\*

The next morning, Camelot woke up to confusion. Not mild confusion, deep, structural, kingdom-wide disarray.

The guards at the castle gates stood arguing with each other over whether today was a patrol day or a parade day and who was going to clean out the armoury. Merchants crowded in the courtyard, shouting at one another about missing permits and licences. The bakery hadn't opened. The stable hands were on strike because someone said Martha said they were not needed any more. The villagers claimed Arthur had promised them all a feast. Guinevere insisted she had a diplomatic visit. And someone had painted a large, ominous question mark on the Round Table.

Arthur stood in the middle of it all, clutching at his temples.

Martha hurried into the courtyard. "How bad is it?" she asked.

Arthur groaned. "It is... a multi-layered crisis of indecision, misinformation, and poor problem solving."

"So... just another normal day then?" Martha replied hopefully.

Arthur gave her a grim look. "No. This is much worse."

Everywhere they looked, people were: stopped in mid-task, unsure of what to do, doing the wrong tasks, doing the same tasks at different times, arguing about what the task even was.

Lancelot approached Arthur nervously with a further problem. "My lord," he said, "no one knows whose turn it is to clean the armoury. So, no one has done it. For three months."

Martha shuddered. "That's... horrifying."

Arthur nodded. "Yes. This is what happens when a kingdom loses its ability to decide what needs to be done."

He turned to Martha. "This is your lesson for today," he said. "We will fix all of Camelot."

Martha scoffed. "I cannot fix a whole kingdom!"

Arthur smiled faintly. "No, Martha. But together... we will teach the kingdom how to fix itself."

Martha looked at the chaos around her. "Well… it is either that, or we move out."

Arthur raised Excalibur high. The ruby blazed, projecting a giant glowing diagram over the courtyard floor.

Villagers gasped. Knights stared. The goose fainted.

The diagram on the floor displayed:

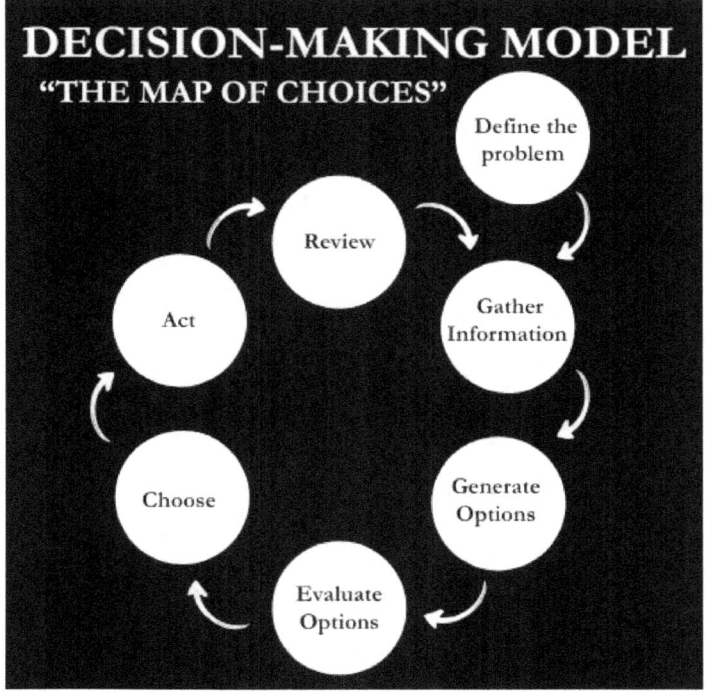

Martha squinted. "It looks like a treasure map."

Arthur nodded. "That's because solving a problem is a treasure hunt, except the treasure is clarity."

She thought about that. "Can I keep it?"

"No, Martha."

"Fine," she shrugged. "How will I remember then?"

Arthur raised the sword again and another vision appeared in the air above them. "By doing it one step at a time," he said. "Now, let us start with... **Step One - *define the problem*.**"

He pointed to the chaos of Camelot. "What is the problem?" he said earnestly.

Martha looked around. Every person she saw was arguing, or standing doing nothing. "Oh! I know!" she said. "No one is doing anything!"

Arthur smiled. "Correct."

The villagers cheered loudly. They were not sure why, but Martha had got something right.

Arthur called the knights forward for... **Step Two - *gather information*.** "This requires order," he said. "Each of you will explain *one* thing. What is happening, and *why*?"

Gawain pushed forward. "The guards refuse to patrol because Percival told them today was parade rehearsal."

Percival looked offended. "It is parade rehearsal!"

"No, it isn't!" shouted Tristan. "Well... maybe... unless it was yesterday..."

Martha whispered, "This is worse than the kitchen."

Arthur whispered back, "Everything right now is worse than the kitchen, Martha."

Arthur raised the sword again. A new glowing vision appeared on the wall.

> ## CAUSE vs SYMPTOM
> **Symptom:** The guards stopped patrolling
> **Cause:** They were told not to patrol
> **Underlying cause:** A message error
> **Root cause:** No unified schedule

Martha gasped. "It is the calendar again!"

Arthur nodded grimly. "Camelot is overly dependent on a single, extremely badly kept calendar."

Percival stepped forward indignantly. "It is a beautiful calendar!"

"Yes," Arthur agreed. "With lovely drawings. But no logic."

He glared at him.

Arthur turned to Martha. "Let us get on with… **Step Three - *generate options*.**"

"Time for the Thinking Hats," she said, pleased with herself. "Do we make new ones?"

"No," Arthur said quickly. "We can just pretend that we have them on."

## White Hat - *Facts*

Martha, acting out with her invisible white hat on, declared: the guards are confused, the villagers are confused, the knights are confused, Guinevere is confused, and the calendar is confusing.

Arthur nodded. "Excellent factual summary."

## Red Hat - *Feelings*

Cissy spoke through tears, "I feel completely overwhelmed!"

Eve added, "I feel responsible, as if it is all my fault!"

Alice added, "I feel like the goose is judging me!"

The goose honked. It was judging, as it always did.

## Black Hat - *Caution*

Morag growled in her best pessimistic growling voice. "This chaos has delayed everything. It is unsafe for everyone not knowing what is happening. We are all doomed. It is inefficient. And the armoury will soon attract insects. If that's not cleaned out, everyone will get sick, and then they will all die."

Arthur nodded. "That is a legitimate risk analysis, I guess."

## Yellow Hat - *Optimism*

"Well… um… at least no one is injured?" Alice chirped up.

Eve added helpfully, "And the armoury smells better than usual. It took six months to clear it last time!"

Arthur closed his eyes. "Not ideal… but acceptable."

## Green Hat - *Creativity*

Galahad strode forward. "What if we create a giant calendar and clock in the sky that tells everyone what to do and when?"

Arthur coughed politely. "Perhaps… something less apocalyptic."

Lancelot offered, "What if we created a… messenger charm? Something that updates everyone magically?"

Merlin perked up. "I could create a spell for that!"

Arthur immediately shook his head violently. "No spells."

Merlin sulked.

## Blue Hat - *Control/Process*

Arthur, who just so happened to have the giant blue mixing bowl under his arm, popped it on his head and summarised: Camelot needs a unified method of communication. We need a decision-making structure. And... we need to fix the calendar.

Martha raised her hand. "Oh! I have an idea too!"

Arthur braced.

"We make a *new* calendar! One that makes sense! With colours! And sections! And... boxes!"

Arthur blinked slowly. "...Martha. That is... *brilliant*."

Martha glowed. "I know!"

Arthur raised his sword again as **Step Four** was about to move into action, ***evaluate options***.

A giant glowing picture appeared:

## DECISION MAKING MATRIX

| Option | Benefit | Risk | Effort | Score |
|---|---|---|---|---|
| **A** Giant Sky Clock | High Drama | Extremely Dangerous | Impossible | NO |
| **B** Magic Messenger Spell | Fast | Potentially Catastrophic | Merlin - Related | ABSOLUTELY NOT |
| **C** New Unified Calendar | Clear | Minimal Risk | Moderate Effort | **YES** |
| **D** Keep Current Chaos | Familiar | Terrible | Easy | NO |

Martha clapped. "We pick C!"

And with that, **Step Five - *choose***, was also completed.

Arthur nodded proudly. "So, we choose C. And now **Step Six - *act*.**"

Arthur handed Martha a fresh parchment. "Martha. Build it."

She flinched. "*Me*?!"

"Yes. You used to avoid decisions. Now you will make one of the kingdom's biggest."

She inhaled. Her quill hovered. She drew a long vertical line, then seven neat horizontal lines. She labelled days. Times. Tasks. People. Places. She created: colour-coded duties, clear symbols for knights, villagers, maids, and cooks, mealtimes, opening hours for stallholders, patrol times and parade times, training times, royal diplomatic events, rest periods and lunch breaks, or brunch. And Feast and festive days.

Arthur watched in awe. "Martha… this is… structured."

She blushed. "I know. I am frightened too."

When she finished, Arthur held it up. The knights applauded. The villagers cheered. The goose honked respectfully.

Percival gasped. "It is beautiful."

Arthur smiled. "It is practical."

Martha whispered, "It is *mine*."

Arthur hung the calendar on the main castle outside wall with a ceremonial nail so that everyone in Camelot could see it. The moment it was posted: guards found their patrol times, villagers found their appointments to renew licences, knights found their training rotations, the market found its opening schedule, the stables found their feeding times, Guinevere found that she was not allowed to change the schedule, everyone knew when the armoury needed cleaning out.

Camelot... began to function. People nodded. People were organised. People moved about with purpose.

Martha stared in awe. "Did... I... do that?"

Arthur nodded. "Yes."

And then the unthinkable happened...

Morag said, "Well done!, Martha."

Martha nearly fainted.

Arthur projected one final glowing message:

**Step Seven, *review*.**

Martha looked at the kingdom. It was calmer, organised, functional. "I never thought I'd say this," she whispered, "but solving problems is… fun," she said, as everyone turned tail and headed home for the evening.

\*\*\*\*\*

Camelot's new calendar had only been on the wall for one day when disaster struck.

The next morning, just after dawn, three things all happened at once:

1. A travelling merchant caravan arrived, demanding entry.
2. The southern bridge collapsed, apparently from age, not sabotage, though sabotage was loudly suspected.
3. The royal messenger returned breathlessly with a scroll declaring that a neighbouring lord wanted to visit, today.

Arthur read the scroll once.

Martha read it twice, having misread it the first time, and panicked. "Oh no. *Oh no.* Three big things. All today!"

Arthur nodded. "Yes. Camelot faces competing priorities. This is the greatest training test of decision-making for you today, Martha."

Martha folded her arms. "Well, someone better decide something quick before everything explodes again like the cauldron."

Arthur looked directly at her. "Martha... you are that someone."

She blinked. "Oh no. *No, no, no.* No thank you. I did it all yesterday."

"Yes, Martha. It is time to do it all over again today. Problems and decision-making don't just happen once. They are happening all the time," Arthur said solemnly.

Arthur summoned his whole leadership circle, the knights, Guinevere, Morag, Cissy, Eve, Alice, the castle steward, a few confused villagers, Merlin, who actually invited himself, and the goose, who basically refused to leave.

They all gathered in the Great Hall. The atmosphere was tense.

Arthur raised his hand. "Camelot must decide which of three critical issues to prioritise, the merchants, the fallen bridge, or the diplomatic visit. We cannot do all three at once."

The room erupted in instant conflict.

"The merchants bring goods!"

"But the bridge is vital!"

"But the lord's visit could be an alliance!"

"But the merchants are angry!"

"But the bridge is dangerous!"

"But the lord has a temper!"

"But the merchants have camels!"

"But the bridge has a troll!"

Arthur cleared his throat. "Yes, there is also apparently a troll now."

Martha whispered to him, "Was he always there?"

Arthur shrugged. "Trolls come and go, like most CEOs."

Arthur lifted Excalibur. The ruby glowed. A new diagram appeared that Martha had kind of seen before in a previous lesson, but she was sure it was slightly formatted differently. To the others, it was something completely new and exciting.

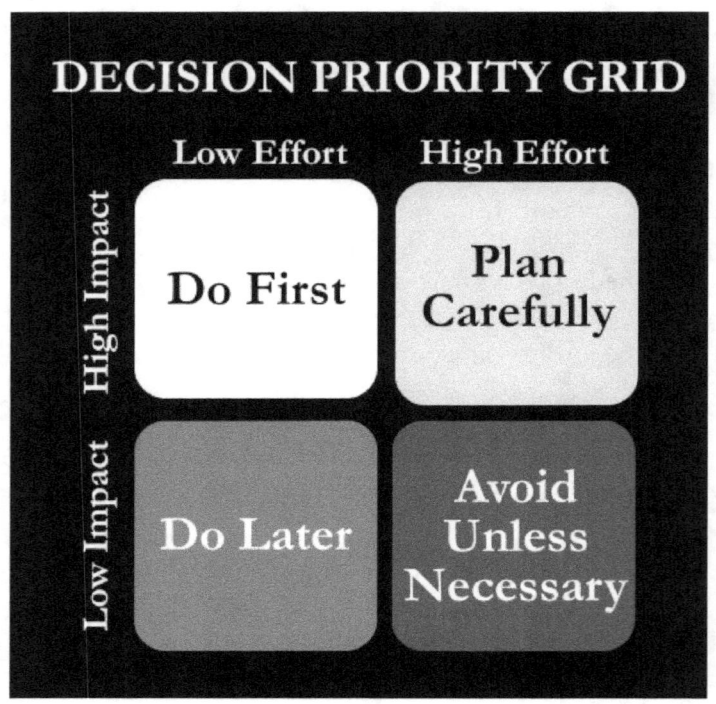

**DECISION PRIORITY GRID**

| | Low Effort | High Effort |
|---|---|---|
| **High Impact** | Do First | Plan Carefully |
| **Low Impact** | Do Later | Avoid Unless Necessary |

The knights squinted. Gawain asked, "Can we strike at it?"

"No," Arthur sighed.

Lancelot asked, "Can we charm it?"

"No."

Eve asked, "Can it explode?"

"NO."

Martha's eyes widened. "It is like the Eisenhower Matrix's cousin!" she exclaimed, remembering now where she had seen it before. "Everything fits together so nicely."

"Yes, yes it does, and *yes*, it is like a cousin," Arthur said proudly. "And now we shall use it for this." Arthur stepped back. "Martha. Lead the session."

Martha squeaked. "*Me*?!"

"Yes. Camelot needs a leader who understands structured thinking."

"I cannot do it!" she said, blushing.

"Martha... you've already done root cause, hats, matrices, and brainstorming."

She paused. "Oh! Yes. I have." She clapped loudly. "Right, everyone. We're doing Structured Decision-Making."

Morag muttered, "That sounds painful."

## Step 1 - *Define the Decision*

Martha pointed at the three crises listed on a large parchment:

1. Merchant caravan demanding entry
2. Southern bridge collapse
3. Diplomatic visit

"Which *must* we handle first?"

The crowd murmured anxiously.

## Step 2 - *Criteria Setting*

Martha cleared her throat dramatically. "We need... criteria!"

Arthur nodded approvingly. "Good. That is a very mature new step."

Martha wrote:
- Safety
- Economic impact
- Political importance
- Time sensitivity
- Resources required

The knights gasped at Martha's wisdom.

"This woman has grown powerful," Bedivere murmured.

Arthur smiled. "She's taking everything she is learning and making it her own."

## Step 3 - *Evaluate Each Crisis*

Martha held her quill like a weapon.

BRIDGE
Safety risk - *HIGH*
Economic risk - *HIGH*
Time sensitivity - *MEDIUM*
Effort - *HIGH*

Everyone nodded. Political risk did not really come into the equation this time. "And now for the merchant caravan?" she said.

Morag answered, "They're loud, impatient, and blocking the road."

Gawain added, "One of them shouted at me."

"That's just people, Gawain," Tristan said gently.

Martha scribbled:

> MERCHANT CARAVAN
> Safety risk - *LOW*
> Economic risk - *HIGH*
> Political risk - *LOW*
> Time sensitivity - *HIGH*
> Effort - *MEDIUM*

"And the diplomatic visit?" she asked.

Guinevere strutted forward. "He is a very important lord."

Morag muttered, "He is a very annoying lord."

Lancelot added, "He once cried because someone looked at him directly."

Martha scribbled:

> DIPLOMATIC VISIT
> Safety risk - *LOW*
> Economic risk - *MEDIUM*
> Political risk - *VERY HIGH*
> Time sensitivity - *TODAY*
> Effort - *LOW* to *MEDIUM*

Arthur nodded. "Now... we choose," he said with valour.

Martha popped a blue mixing bowl on her head dramatically.

## Step 4 - *The Blue Hat Moment, Decision*

"Blue Hat means decision time!" she yelled.

Arthur whispered, "You don't need the hat."

Martha whispered back, "I want the hat."

She stood tall. "Based on criteria... we handle the *bridge first.*"

The hall erupted into a chorus of voices.

"The merchants will be furious!"

"The lord will be insulted!"

"The troll will be delighted!"

"The trade route will suffer!"

"The bridge supports everything!"

Martha lifted her hand. "Wait!" Silence fell.

"We fix the bridge *first* because if the bridge collapses further, *no one* gets in or out, *no* trade comes, *no* lord arrives safely, and *we fall into a ravine with the troll.*"

Guinevere blinked slowly. "Oh. Well, when you put it like that…"

Arthur smiled. "She is correct."

## Step 5 - *Create the Action Plan*

Martha arranged each group as follows, to be dispatched accordingly:

- Bridge Team: Morag, Gawain, Ector, Eve (supervised), one very confused donkey
- Merchant Team: Tristan, Lancelot, Percival, Alice (with strict instructions not to touch anything)
- Diplomatic Team: Guinevere, Bedivere, two castle maids, the goose (Guinevere insisted)

At the bridge, the team discovered:
- The wood was rotten
- The support beams had cracked
- The troll had been "borrowing" planks
- Eve had accidentally loosened a bolt last week while "investigating noises"

Martha muttered, "Root cause… Eve again."

Eve raised her hand apologetically. "I genuinely did not mean it. There was a funny noise."

Morag growled. "We'll fix it. Together."

The bridge team rebuilt, reinforced, corrected measurements, and for once, made zero fires.

Martha was stunned. "They're… co-operating."

Arthur nodded. "Because you made a decision."

The team looking after the merchants arrived where they were located. Tristan approached the merchants with tea. Lancelot approached with charm. Percival approached with paperwork. Alice approached with fear.

The merchants softened. "*Ah!* A team that knows what it is doing!"

Alice whispered, "Do we?"

Tristan smiled. "Of course we do."

They negotiated delayed entry until the bridge was secure. Progress here was agreed and made.

The diplomatic team, led now by Guinevere, greeted the lord with:
- Over-the-top politeness
- Under-the-table bribery
- A goose wearing a bow tie

The lord was so overwhelmed he forgot to be offended.

Bedivere whispered privately to Arthur later, "It was the goose in the bow tie that saved us."

Arthur nodded solemnly. "What's good for the goose is good for the gander!"

## Step 6 - Review

That evening, everyone in Camelot gathered again.

Arthur lifted his sword. The ruby projected:

Martha stared. "I… did that?"

Arthur nodded. "Yes, Martha. You applied every part of the problem-solving cycle."

Her eyes shone. "I did not panic."

"No."

"I did not hide."

"No."

"Martha," he said gently, "you are learning to solve problems, not by instinct, but by structure."

Martha placed a hand on her chest. "It feels… very powerful."

"It is powerful," Arthur said. "And you will need that power next week."

She frowned. "What's next week?"

Arthur's face darkened. "Conflict Management & Difficult Conversations."

Martha gasped. "Oh no. People who are angry."

Arthur nodded solemnly. "And you will have to talk to all of them."

Martha whimpered softly.

The goose in the bow tie, who had made a run from the diplomat, honked sympathetically.

# CHAPTER SEVEN

## In Which Everyone Has A
## Point, And No One Is Happy
### Conflict Management &
### Difficult Conversations

The day, once again, began with shouting. This was not unusual, as Gawain shouted almost every morning when he found someone else polishing his armour "incorrectly", but today the shouting echoed through the entire castle.

Arthur hurried to the courtyard. Three knights were arguing. Two villagers were arguing. The maids were frosty with each other, and Guinevere was arguing with Barnaby the goat over a bunch of flowers he was casually eating. And in the middle of it all stood Martha, clutching a broom defensively, like someone attempting to fight off a swarm of bees.

Arthur approached her carefully. "Martha… what on earth has happened?"

She pointed helplessly. "Everyone is angry. Everyone is angry at everyone."

Arthur surveyed the courtyard.

A knight shouted, "You stole my horse!"

Another shouted, "You said I could borrow it!"

A villager cried, "You stepped on my turnips and damaged my aubergine!"

"I did not see them!"

"You should look where you're walking!"

Guinevere yelled at Barnaby, "Stop eating my favourite peonies!"

Barnaby, being Barnaby, remained silent and continued to munch.

Martha whimpered. "Arthur, I hate conflict. Can we not just send everyone back to bed?"

Arthur shook his head. "No, Martha. This is your next lesson."

She groaned. "Why is leadership so full of… people?"

Arthur patted her shoulder sympathetically. "That, Martha, is precisely the problem. If people were not involved as our staff and customers, then leadership would be easy, but it is not like that, unfortunately."

Arthur lifted Excalibur. The ruby glowed brightly and projected a large glowing diagram across the courtyard, causing people to pause mid-argument.

Some villagers gasped. Gawain ducked for cover. Barnaby bleated rather enthusiastically.

The projection displayed:

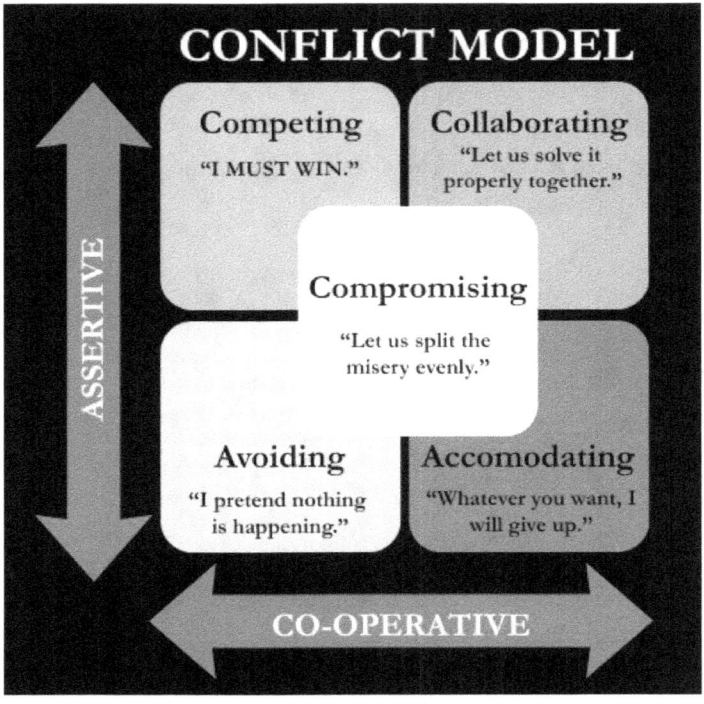

Martha pointed. "Oh! That one," she jabbed at **Avoiding**, "that's me! That's what I do when Morag yells!"

Arthur nodded. "Indeed."

She pointed at **Competing**. "And that's Gawain."

The courtyard all nodded as one.

She pointed at **Accommodating**. "That's Tristan, bless him."

Tristan held up a tray of tea and biscuits. "I just want everyone to be happy."

She pointed at **Compromising**. "That's Bedivere."

Bedivere nodded. "I negotiate on everything. Once I negotiated on the price of a non-slip banana peel, and I and the price went tumbling."

Finally, she pointed at **Collaborating**. "Does... anyone here *do* that?"

The courtyard was silent. Even Barnaby bowed his head in shame.

Arthur sighed. "That is why we train and learn."

Arthur raised the sword again. A new projection appeared, shaped like a square, showing behaviours everyone was well aware of:

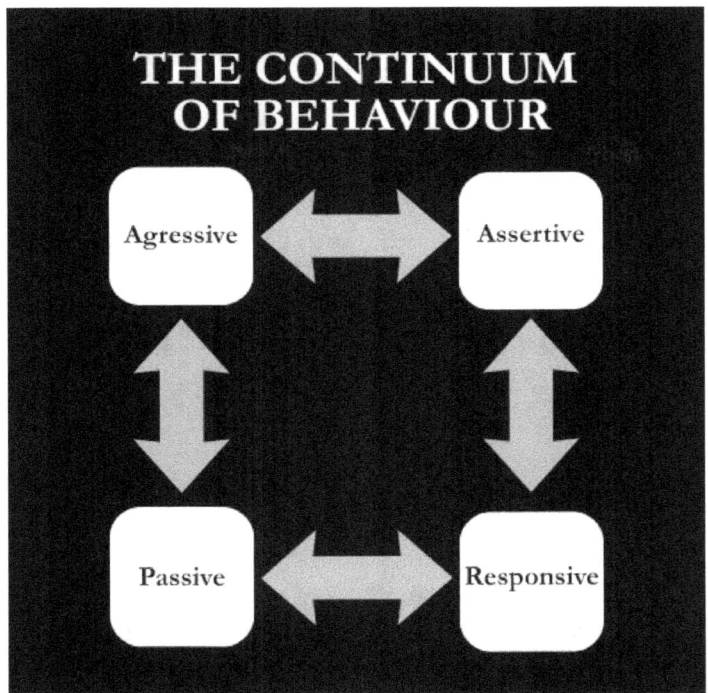

THE CONTINUUM
OF BEHAVIOUR

Agressive ⟷ Assertive

Passive ⟷ Responsive

The crowd murmured.

Martha squinted. "It is like a behaviour sausage going in all directions!"

Arthur blinked slowly. "...Yes, Martha. A sausage of behaviour."

He pointed to the bottom left-hand corner.

"Here we have **Passive** people," he said. "This type of behaviour is characterised by staying quiet, avoiding conflict and discussions, hoping that things will just go away. The trouble is, people who display this behaviour often find their needs are not met. We call them 'BOHICAS' on the battlefield."

Tristan raised a timid hand. "Oh dear. That's me at times."

"What is a *Bohica*?" asked Martha, totally intrigued as to why Tristan would acknowledge being one.

Arthur laughed. "It is a mnemonic," he said, "the letters stand for **B**end **O**ver, **H**ere **I**t **C**omes **A**gain, or **BOHICA** for short."

Martha looked quizzically at Tristan, who blushed and offered her a chocolate Hobnob.

"In the top left," Arthur resumed before any further questions were asked, "are the **Aggressive** people, who themselves believe they are not angry all the time, but they shout, stare, glare, call people rude names, slam doors, and leave little notes lying around to annoy others."

Guinevere stiffened. "I DO NOT DO THAT, YOU STUPID MAN!" she yelled.

Arthur arched an eyebrow and pulled a post-it note from his pocket, amazingly, as they had not been invented yet. Written on it, in Guinevere's handwriting, was a note telling him to walk Barnaby this morning before breakfast and feed him, please. "Oh," Arthur said suddenly, "it says 'Please'. Sorry, I thought it said 'Peonies'."

Guinevere crossed her arms dramatically, stared straight at Barnaby, who had by now finished his so-called breakfast, and continued to glare at him without blinking.

Martha whispered to Arthur, "Yep. That's pretty aggressive to me."

"In the bottom right-hand corner are the **Responsive** people," Arthur continued. "Responsive people are characterised by being in the moment, exploring things internally, and not always finding the right words straight away. They are excellent listeners, show empathy, and ask questions, but do not always have the answers."

Martha pointed at the glowing word Responsive. "So, this is a good one?"

Arthur nodded. "Yes. You cannot be assertive to resolve conflict if you don't demonstrate responsive behaviours first."

"Finally," he said, pointing at the top right-hand corner, "are **Assertive** people."

"Assertive people," he continued, "know what their needs are and how to obtain them without interfering with the rights and needs of others."

Gawain roared, "Well, that sounds tricky. Who wins if we both acknowledge each other's needs and rights?"

Barnaby bleated once more, as if telling Gawain to be quiet.

Gawain snapped, "The goat is wrong!"

Arthur sighed. "Yes, Barnaby. Gawain is being aggressive," he said, patting the goat's head. Arthur held up his hand to two villagers arguing over a sack of potatoes nearby. "Observe," he said to Martha.

The villagers froze, confused but obedient.

Arthur whispered to them, "Enact each behaviour in order."

They nodded.

**Passive**

Villager 1 (whispering): "You can have the potatoes. It is fine."

Villager 2: "Really?"

Villager 1: "Yes. I… did not want them anyway."

Villager 2: Leaves happily.

Villager 1: Bursts into tears.

Martha gasped. "Oh no! He gave away his potatoes *and* his happiness!"

Arthur nodded. "That is the cost of passivity."

**Aggressive**

Villager 1 (with a cold smile): "No, no, *you* take the potatoes. It is *fine*." (Places potatoes on the ground harshly.) "I hope they make you *happy*, and I hope *your* soup burns."

Martha recoiled. "Oh. I know *that* one," she said, glancing at Guinevere.

Guinevere bristled and huffed loudly.

**Responsive**

Villager 1: "I know we both need the potatoes. How many do you need?"

Villager 2: "Probably just three or four."

Villager 1: "You might need more than that. How about I give you five of mine?"

Villager 2: "That is very kind of you, thank you."
(Quietly wishing he had asked for more.)

The crowd applauded.

**Assertive**

Villager 1: Took a breath and spoke clearly. "I need these potatoes for my family's dinner today. But I know you also need some. We shall divide the sack equally."

Villager 2: Nodded. "That sounds very fair."

They shared the potatoes evenly.

Everyone in the courtyard cheered at the novelty of what they had witnessed.

Arthur turned to Martha. "That is what assertiveness looks like."

Martha whispered, "It is… beautiful."

Just as Arthur prepared to move on to difficult conversations, a knight sprinted into the courtyard. "My lord! The blacksmith and the baker are at war!"

Arthur's eyes widened. "Actual war?"

The knight nodded. "They're throwing bread and horseshoes at each other."

The courtyard winced.

Arthur sighed. "Martha… your lesson in conflict management begins now."

She squealed. "Oh no. Why could it not be something easier? Like wrestling an alligator? Or solving a murder on a Thursday, like Richard Osman will do in the future?"

Arthur gestured sternly. "Come. This is your destiny."

Martha muttered as she followed, "I don't want this destiny. I want a smaller one. With fewer people in it."

When they reached the market, chaos awaited:
- The baker (Hugh) was red-faced and furious
- The blacksmith (Roderick) was holding a burnt loaf
- Bread was scattered on the ground
- A horseshoe lay embedded in a pile of dough

- A dog was eating something it absolutely should not eat
- The villagers had gathered to watch, delighted

Hugh shouted, "YOU STOLE MY FIREWOOD!"

Roderick yelled, "YOU BLOCKED MY FORGE DOOR!"

Hugh shouted louder, "**YOU OVERCHARGED ME FOR FLOUR!**"

Roderick bellowed, "**YOU BURNT MY WIFE'S FAVOURITE PIE!**"

Arthur stepped forward. "Martha. This is your conversation to deal with."

Martha froze. "*What*?!"

"You must mediate. Using assertiveness."

She trembled. "I cannot!"

Arthur whispered, "Yes, you can."

Martha inhaled, turned to both men, lifted her trembling broom, and said, "*Stop this!*"

Shockingly, they did.

She swallowed hard. "Right. We are going to have a difficult conversation. Without shouting. Without bread throwing. Without horseshoes. And without… whatever that dog is eating." She gently removed something from the dog's mouth. It honked really badly. "First," Martha said, "everyone gets *one* turn to speak. Assertively."

Hugh shouted first, "I…"

"No shouting," Martha said firmly. "Assertiveness only, please. We will not have any aggression in our conversation."

He took a breath. "I feel frustrated because I need wood and flour for baking, and Roderick has taken away my supply of wood and has charged me too much for the flour."

Roderick blinked. "That is… partly true," he said.

Martha nodded. "Good. Now you continue, Roderick."

Roderick cleared his throat. "I feel overwhelmed. My forge is overworked, with everyone using it for baking bread, and Hugh leaves flour and wood everywhere. My door often gets stuck, which causes the heat to rise inside, and my horseshoes bend out of shape."

Martha beamed. "You're both being honest! And no one is dying! Look at this progress!"

Arthur whispered, "This is going strangely well."

She turned back. "Now we find the solution."

They stared at her. She waited. Nothing.

She sighed. "Fine. We brainstorm."

Arthur braced himself.

Martha raised her hands, and Arthur raised his sword slightly without anyone seeing. A projection appeared:

> **RULE 1: No judging ideas while they're being spoken.**
>
> **RULE 2: Only one idea at a time.**
>
> **RULE 3: Everyone must contribute.**

Martha, who surprised herself, read the vision aloud to everyone. "Do we understand?" she asked, as the vision disappeared in front of them all.

They nodded.

Hugh offered, "We could share wood deliveries."

Roderick offered, "I would adjust my prices if flour doesn't get everywhere."

A villager offered, "We could build a better shared storage shed."

Eve offered, "What if we bought flour that wasn't flammable?"

Arthur said, "Eve, please stop."

Alice offered, "We could create a schedule for oven time!"

Martha gasped. "*Yes*! Collaborative scheduling!"

She turned to Arthur, glowing. "I solved it!"

He corrected softly, "No, Martha. They solved it. You facilitated it."

Her chest swelled. "Oh. That's... even better."

Arthur raised the sword for the final time that day. The ruby projected:

# CONFLICT MANAGEMENT
## KEY LEARNINGS

**Conflict styles differ**
**Behaviour patterns matter**
**Assertiveness is healthiest**
**Process beats shouting**
**Listening solves more than winning**
**Mediation requires structure**
**Difficult conversations can strengthen relationships**

Martha stared at it long and hard. "Arthur... I did not faint. I did not run. I did not hide behind Barnaby and," she continued proudly, "I had a difficult conversation!"

Arthur nodded. "Yes, Martha. And tomorrow... you will, I am sure, have another."

Martha squealed. "No, once is enough!"

Arthur smiled as everyone went about their things for the rest of the day.

*****

The next morning, the marketplace was still recovering from yesterday's bread and horseshoe war. Surprisingly, though, it had been astonishingly calm for most of the morning. Which often meant something terrible was about to happen. Arthur sensed it. Martha sensed it. Even Barnaby sensed it.

The calm snapped when two knights burst into the courtyard, shouting accusations at each other.

Tristan peeked out from behind a pillar. "Oh dear," he whispered. "It is starting again."

The knights in question were Sir Kay and Sir Gareth, both normally tolerable until provoked, and both now very much provoked.

"YOU STOLE MY PRACTICE SWORD!" Kay roared.

"I DID NOT STEAL IT!" Gareth shouted back. "YOU HAVE MISPLACED IT!"

"YOU ALWAYS BLAME ME!"

"YOU ALWAYS ASSUME THE WORST!"

Arthur sighed. "Martha," he said gently, "today's lesson begins here."

Arthur raised Excalibur. The ruby shot out a soft blue light, not the fiery red of emergencies, but the cool glow of learning about people's emotional dysfunction. A glowing vision in blue appeared above the courtyard:

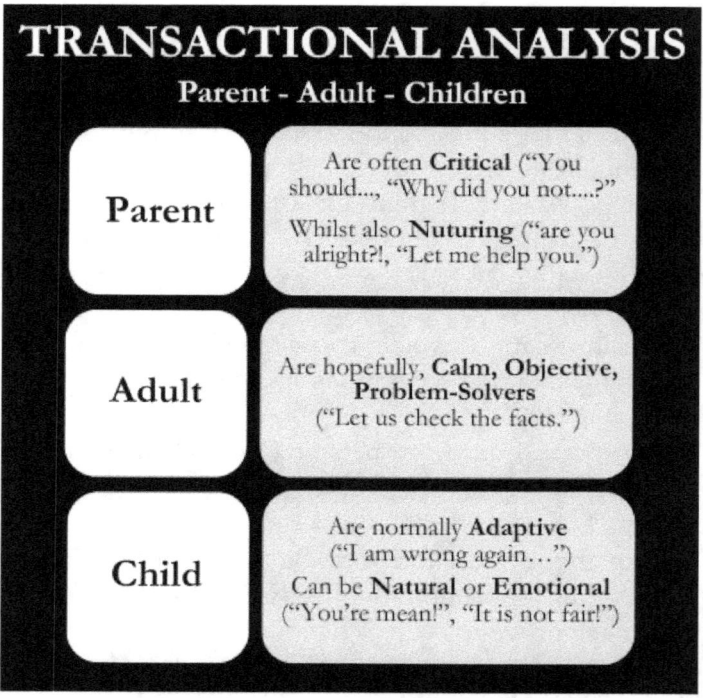

# TRANSACTIONAL ANALYSIS
## Parent - Adult - Children

| | |
|---|---|
| **Parent** | Are often **Critical** ("You should...", "Why did you not....?") Whilst also **Nuturing** ("are you alright?!, "Let me help you.") |
| **Adult** | Are hopefully, **Calm, Objective, Problem-Solvers** ("Let us check the facts.") |
| **Child** | Are normally **Adaptive** ("I am wrong again...") Can be **Natural** or **Emotional** ("You're mean!", "It is not fair!") |

Martha tilted her head. "What's that?" she asked.

Arthur cleared his throat. "This, Martha, is Transactional Analysis. It is a model that will come to pass in around 1957 from a Canadian gentleman named **Eric Berne**. It shows how people speak from different states of mind."

He pointed to the diagram and explained.

Martha's eyes widened. "Oh! So, people *literally* talk like their parents or their inner children?"

Arthur nodded. "Exactly. Conflict erupts when two people communicate from clashing states." He gestured at the feuding knights.

Kay: "You *always* take my things!" → **Critical Parent**

Gareth: "You're *always* picking on me!" → **Frustrated Child**

Martha gasped. "They're not even arguing like adults!"

Arthur nodded. "No one in Camelot argues like an adult." Then he whispered, "Martha, can you explain to me Kay's state?"

She squinted. "He's being a Parent, but a very bad version of one. Like my Aunt Agatha used to be, when she did not like my soup."

Arthur nodded. "And Gareth?"

Martha raised her hand proudly. "A Child! An angry one! Probably needs a nap or more sugar."

Arthur gave a small smile. "You are learning."

The ruby projection flickered and changed the image. A glowing diagram now showed little pictures of swords, horseshoes, bread rolls, goats, and flowers, each shooting little bolts of light.

**EMOTIONAL TRIGGERS**

Feeling ignored

Feeling blamed

Feeling unsafe

Feeling disrespected

Feeling powerless

Martha frowned. "What is *that*?"

Arthur explained, "People react badly when certain things hit their 'hot buttons'. As we saw with Barnaby and Guinevere and the Peonies for Breakfast and again between Hugh and Roderick with their Horse Shoes and Bread disagreements."

Arthur turned to the knights. "Kay's trigger," he said softly, "is losing control. Gareth's is being blamed."

Martha gasped. "They're not really angry about the sword!"

"Exactly."

She whispered dramatically, "It is a metaphor sword!"

Arthur gently corrected, "It is literally a sword. But yes."
Arthur nudged her forward. "Go on. Try calming them."

She hesitated. "What if they yell at me?"

"They will."

"What if they hit me?"

"They will not."

Martha stepped between the knights.

"STOP THIS PLEASE!" she yelled.

Kay and Gareth froze.

She lowered her voice. "Right. Now tell me what's really bothering you."

Kay huffed, "He *never* listens to me."

Gareth snapped, "He *always* talks down to me."

Martha nodded sagely. "Oh. It sounds like you're both being emotional toddlers to me."

Arthur whispered, "Close enough, I guess. It needs a little refinement."

He raised Excalibur once more, and a new structure appeared:

Martha's jaw dropped. "This is like... a recipe for talking!"

Arthur nodded. "Yes. A conversation recipe, developed in years to come by **Sharon and Gordon Bower**."

"Well, why did you not say that? I love recipes. Do Sharon and Gordon create any others in the future?"

Arthur rubbed his eyes. "Yes, Martha, I should have known you would like a recipe, and I don't know what they went on to do in the future."

She turned to the knights. "OK, no worries. Now then, you two. We're going to do this DESC thing."

Arthur whispered, "Maybe don't yell the word 'DESC' like a battle cry."

She continued in a softer tone. "Kay, you go first."

Kay straightened, a little confused, but obedient.

Martha coached him through the structure, mouthing the words for him to say, and he followed along nicely:

**D** - *Describe The Behaviour*
"I saw you borrow my practice sword without asking."

**E** - *Express Impact*
"It makes me feel disrespected and out of control."

**S** - *Specify What You Want*
"I want you to ask my permission next time."

**C** - *Consequences*
"If you do that, we'll avoid arguments in the future."

Gareth nodded. "That... was... reasonable," he said, stunned.

Martha squealed quietly. "Arthur! It is working!"

Arthur nodded. "Good. Now Gareth."

She guided him too, in exactly the same way:

**D** - *Describe The Behaviour*
"You accuse me of wrongdoing before checking facts."

**E** - *Express Impact*
"That makes me feel unfairly blamed."

**S** - *Specify What You Want*
"I want you to ask me calmly before yelling at me."

**C** - *Consequences*
"Then I will cooperate with you faster."

Kay gasped. "That was... actually helpful," he said, shrugging.

Arthur smiled. "Notice how assertive communication defuses conflict."

Martha clapped. "This is brilliant!"

Kay muttered, "So… we're not fighting anymore?"

Gareth shrugged. "I guess not."

Just then, Eve sprinted into the courtyard, waving a smoking ladle. "Martha! Alice said to me the stew wasn't salty enough, so I put in more salt, but she said I over-salted it, so I told her if she could do it better, then do it herself… and she said I always ruin things and threw a potato at me, and I think we are now fighting!"

Alice chased in behind her, brandishing a potato masher. "Martha!" Alice screeched. "Eve dumped half a barrel of salt into the stew, and now it tastes like the ocean is angry!"

Arthur muttered, "Perfect timing."

Martha took a deep breath. "All right, you two. We're going to solve this little conflict once and for all," she said in a stern, matter-of-fact way.

Arthur whispered, "Good, Martha. Shine the light on what it is, conflict!"

Eve and Alice froze immediately.

Martha turned towards them, both still glaring at each other across the courtyard like two feral cats fighting over the same fish. Eve clutched her smoking ladle. Alice clutched her potato masher with the intensity of someone considering war.

Martha inhaled slowly. "Right... you two. It is DESC time."

Eve blinked. "*Desc?* Desc what?"

Alice snapped, "I *think* it means stop waving the ladle."

Martha raised her broom like a referee's staff. "No. DESC is how we *talk without exploding* at each other. We will go step by step."

Eve let out a nervous giggle. "I panic when Martha says step by step."

Alice hissed, "You panic when anything happens."

Eve gasped dramatically. "That is not true!" and immediately tripped over nothing.

Martha clapped loudly. "Stop! Adult mode, please."

Both cooks froze mid-glare.

Martha guided Eve gently first. "Eve, you'll go through the four steps. I will help you all the way."

Eve nodded shakily.

Martha placed a comforting hand on her shoulder. "OK. Step one."

**D** - *Describe The Behaviour*

Eve faced Alice slowly. "When you said the stew wasn't salty enough," she began, "I... added more salt."

Alice stamped her foot. "YOU ADDED HALF OF THE ENTIRE BARREL!"

Martha held up her hand. "Stop. Describe. Not shout."

Alice folded her arms.

Eve continued, "I added a *lot* of salt because I thought you wanted more."

Alice blinked. "That is... technically accurate."

**E** - *Express The Impact*

"Now," Martha said kindly, "tell Alice how it made you feel."

Eve's lip wobbled. "I felt... undervalued. And stupid. Like I cannot do anything right."

Alice's face softened. "Oh. I... did not know you felt like that."

Eve sniffed loudly. "I did!" Then burst into tears.

Martha sighed. "Good. That's the 'E'. Weepy Eve is allowed."

**S** - *Specify What You Want*

Martha handed Eve a clean piece of cloth. "Now tell her what you want in the future."

Eve straightened, blew her nose on the cloth, and handed it back to Martha. "I want you to tell me clearly how salty something should be. Don't just say 'some'. Say 'this much'. Or use your hands. Or do a drawing."

Martha handed the snotty cloth to Arthur, who gave it to Barnaby to dispose of, or eat.

Alice nodded. "That… makes sense. Actually," she said, watching Barnaby eat the cloth.

## C - *Consequences*
"And now," Martha said, "explain the consequences, please, Eve."

Eve exhaled. "If you do that, I will not over-salt things. And you will not have to chase me with a potato masher."

Alice lowered the masher guiltily. "That's fair enough."

Martha turned to Alice. "Your turn."

Alice took a deep breath. "OK, my turn," she began nervously.

"Yes," Martha encouraged. "Describe first," she said calmly.

Alice pointed dramatically. "Eve, when you dumped half the salt barrel into the stew…"

Eve flinched.

"…the stew tasted like the ocean had been crying salty tears for days."

Martha nodded. "Good metaphor. Continue and express the impact."

"I felt... overwhelmed," Alice admitted. "And I panicked. And I got angry," she said, her face contorting. "And then I threw the potato across the room, because I was..."

Martha tapped her gently. "Emotional surge there. Stay Adult Alice, please, and specify what you want."

Alice deflated. "Right. Sorry." She inhaled again. "I want you to stop panicking when I critique something."

Eve blinked. "Even small critiques?"

"Yes. Because I am not attacking you, I am trying to help us," Alice said with a grin.

Eve's eyes widened. "Oh. I did not know that," she said with a smile.

Martha nodded. "This is good. Now for the consequences!"

Alice sighed. "If we talk calmly, then potatoes will not get thrown. And you will not cry. And Morag will not yell. And Martha will not need to intervene."

Eve blinked. Martha nodded. Then both said, "You're right."

Then Alice and Eve started speaking at once.

"I am so sorry."

"I did not mean to."

"I did not know."

"I should not have."

Martha clapped. "All right. One apology at a time. Let us not regress into childhood chaos."

They both burst into a mix of laughter, tears, and the half–hug–half-shove that uniquely characterises workplace reconciliation.

Martha breathed out deeply. "I think I am... good at this," she whispered, staring in mild awe at the two cooks, now bonding over the earlier argument that was almost forgotten.

Arthur nodded proudly. "You are, Martha. And you're not even armed with a vegetable."

Martha smirked. "Small victories."

Arthur nodded. "Yes. You may never stop having conflict in Camelot, but now you can start to manage it."

Arthur was hoping for a quiet afternoon. Martha was hoping to avoid any people. Camelot, however, had other plans.

Another roar erupted from the outer courtyard, not the roar of battle, but the roar of many voices shouting at once.

Arthur stiffened. "That," he said, "is the sound of a kingdom about to split into pieces."

Martha whimpered. "Oh no. *Oh no.* Are we at war? I am not emotionally ready for war."

Arthur shook his head. "No. Worse. We have... an internal organisational dispute."

Martha squeaked.

The two hurried toward the sound, and what they found was truly impressive. On the left: the villagers, furious, waving tools in the air. On the right: the knights, furious, waving their swords. In the middle: the royal gardeners, looking traumatised.

Lancelot spotted Arthur. "My lord! We need justice!"

A villager shouted, "No! We need justice!"

A gardener cried, "We just need peace and quiet to let the lettuces grow!"

Arthur sighed deeply. "Martha... you know what this means."

She clapped her hands over her ears. "No. *No.* Not again today. I have already done conflict. I have exceeded my quota."

Arthur placed a gentle but firm hand on her shoulder. "This is the ultimate training test. The kingdom needs a mediator. And you are the only one trained to do it."

Martha blinked. "I have only been trained for a couple of days!"

Arthur replied softly, "In Camelot, that makes you an expert."

Martha stepped forward cautiously. "Um… hello… why is everyone shouting here?"

Immediately, three dozen voices screamed at once.

"The knights stole our garden path!"

"They marched through our vegetables!"

"They trampled the spinach!"

"They ruined the radishes!"

"They built it crooked!"

"They did it on purpose!"

Arthur winced. "Martha," he murmured, "ask them to explain one at a time."

"But they're so loud," she whispered.

"Martha," he said calmly, "assertively."

She swallowed. Inhaled. "STOP ALL THIS NOISE, PLEASE. WE CANNOT HEAR EACH OTHER!"

A miracle occurred. Silence.

She lifted her chin, surprised it had worked. "Right. Now. We are going to use structured communication. The first person to explain things will be... Kay."

Kay stepped forward, arms crossed, scowling. "The villagers built a garden path through the training yard *without* permission!"

The villagers erupted again.

Martha raised her hand. "No shouting. The next speaker will try to use an Adult-to-Adult voice."

The villagers shuffled uncertainly.

A woman named Elswith stepped forward. "We did build a path," she admitted, "but only because the knights kept stomping through our vegetable beds and destroying everything. It is not fair!"

The gardeners began to cry again.

"They crushed the cauliflowers!"

"The spinach will never trust us again!"

Arthur closed his eyes. "This," he muttered, "is why empires fall."

Martha frowned. "This is... very silly."

"Silly becomes serious in organisations," Arthur said quietly, "especially when no one knows how to talk to each other."

Martha studied the scene carefully.

Kay: arms crossed, glaring → Critical Parent

Elswith: emotional, accusatory → Child

Gardener Joe: muttering curses → Passive-aggressive Child

Gawain: pacing, shouting → Aggressive Parent

She leaned toward Arthur. "Do we… upgrade them to Adults?"

"Yes," Arthur said. "Immediately."

Martha cleared her throat. "Right. Everyone shift into Adult Mode now."

Blank stares.

"What's Adult Mode?" someone asked.

Martha improvised. "Adult Mode is when you speak calmly, use facts, don't shout, don't blame, don't assume… and stop pulling faces like that." She pointed directly at Gawain. He froze and carefully rearranged his face.

To everyone's astonishment, the group adjusted. The villagers lowered their tools. The knights sheathed their swords. The gardeners stopped sobbing.

Arthur suspected exhaustion played a role, but he accepted the win.

"This," Martha announced, "is now a mediation session."

Elswith raised her hand. "What's mediation?"

Martha puffed up. "It is where we solve conflict without duels, shouting, goats, or weaponised vegetables."

Arthur whispered approvingly, "Clear boundaries. Very good."

## Step One - *Identify Emotional Triggers*

Martha turned to the gardeners first. "What upset you the most?"

Gardener Joe sniffed loudly. "They destroyed our hard work."

Trigger: violation of effort.

She turned to the knights.

Kay admitted, "We felt disrespected. They went behind our backs."

Trigger: loss of control.

Lionel added quietly, "And the path was crooked."

Trigger: perfectionism.

A villager muttered, "They never listen to us."

Trigger: not being heard.

Arthur leaned closer. "You're diagnosing the conflict."

Martha nodded. "Like stew. Too much heat, not enough listening."

## Step Two - *DESC With Both Groups*

Martha did something bold. "All right. We are doing DESC. Together. Knights first. *One* sentence each."

Kay took a breath.
**D**escribe: "When you built the path without telling us…"
**E**xpress: "…we felt ignored."
**S**pecify: "We want discussion before changes."
**C**onsequences: "Then swords remain decorative."

The villagers nodded grudgingly.

Now Elswith spoke.
**D**escribe: "When you trampled our gardens…"
**E**xpress: "…we felt disrespected."
**S**pecify: "We want agreed boundaries."
**C**onsequences: "Then vegetables and tempers survive."

Even the goose honked approval.

Martha whispered to Arthur, "This is actually working."

Arthur smiled softly. "Move quickly before someone ruins it."

## Step Three - *Define The Real Problem*

Arthur projected the truth clearly:

Martha turned to them. "So, the conflict wasn't the path. Or the training. Or the vegetables."

"It was," she said firmly, "that no one talked."

The courtyard gasped. The goose fainted.

**Step Four** - *Generate Solutions*

Martha set the rules.

"No shouting. No blaming. No rejecting ideas immediately."

Suggestions flowed.

"Separate zones!"

"Different training times!"

"A fence!"

"Knights help repair damage!"

Eve raised a hand. "What if we dig a tunnel?"

"No tunnels, Eve," Alice said calmly.

Arthur blinked. "Progress."

## Step Five - *Collaborative Decision*

Martha evaluated calmly:
"Shared schedule – Yes,
Marked training zones – Yes,
Protective fencing – Yes,
Knights help repair gardens – Yes,
Eve's tunnel – No."

Agreement rippled across the courtyard.

Arthur raised Excalibur. The ruby glowed with final clarity:

**CONFLICT RESOLUTION**
**THE TOOLKIT**
Move people to Adult mode
Identify emotional triggers
Use DESC for assertive dialogue
Mediate with structure
Aim for win–win solutions
Clear boundaries prevent repeat conflict

Martha surveyed the transformed courtyard. Knights helped replant vegetables. Villagers marked zones with stones. Gardeners sketched fence ideas and reassured traumatised lettuce.

"I did it," Martha whispered.

Arthur corrected gently. "You led them to do it."

She smiled. "I think… I'm starting to like conflict."

Arthur coughed. "That may be premature."

"Not the conflict," she clarified quickly. "The resolving bit."

"Yes," Arthur agreed. "That makes much more sense."

She looked up. "What's next week?"

Arthur inhaled deeply. "A challenge harder than conflict."

She paled. "Harder than this?"

"Yes. Next week is… Coaching & Developing Others."

Martha screamed as if someone had trampled her tomatoes. And somewhere in the distance, the goose honked ominously.

# CHAPTER EIGHT

## Helping Others Grow
## Without Doing It For Them
### Coaching & Developing Others

Martha was halfway through repairing a broken cupboard door (that she herself had slammed too hard) when Arthur appeared in the doorway of the kitchen. She was, he thought, looking far too serene for someone surrounded by flour, chaos, and the goose wearing a pearl necklace. "Martha," he said gently, "today you learn how to coach."

She blinked at him suspiciously. "Coach what? Horses? Bread? Myself? The goose? Hey, that's Guinevere's necklace, come here, you!" she said, as she ran across the room towards the goose. The goose honked proudly, as if to say, 'Chase me', which was a future catchphrase to come.

Arthur shook his head. "No. Coach people."

Martha froze and turned. "Oh no. *Not people*. People have feelings. People get confused. People whine. People cry. People panic. People..."

Arthur raised a calming hand. "Yes. And you will help them grow."

Martha scowled. "Why can't they grow on their own? Like mould? Or icicles?"

Arthur sighed, the sigh of a tired mentor who had aged twenty years in just a few weeks. "Because," he said, "leadership isn't just about directing tasks. It is developing people so they can become stronger, more capable, and more confident without you."

Martha stared in horror. "So, I'm supposed to... help them, on purpose?"

Arthur nodded. "Yes."

She groaned. "This is going to be worse than conflict."

Arthur chuckled. "That's exactly what most leaders think before learning this skill."

Arthur lifted Excalibur once again and the ruby glowed a vibrant green to signify growth. A new image formed in the air: four large, glowing green letters.

# GROW

Martha tilted her head. "It looks like alphabet spaghetti."

Arthur replied patiently, "It isn't alphabet spaghetti. Besides, that hasn't even been invented yet."

"But it could be. People could have it for brunch with avocado on toast."

"No."

She pointed excitedly at the **'G'**. "Oh! G is for Goose. He still has Guinevere's pearl necklace, where is he?" she said, looking around the kitchen.

"No, Martha. G is for Goal." He pressed the ruby again and the rest of the words appeared:

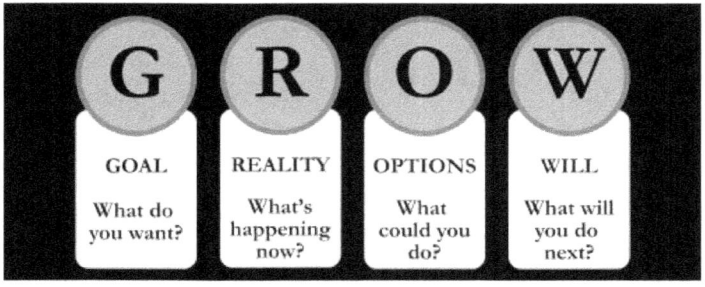

Martha frowned. "And W is actually for... *will* the goose stop wearing the pearl necklace?"

Arthur pinched the bridge of his nose. "Let us... stay focused."

Arthur called to Tristan through the open kitchen window to come in and join them at the Round Table upstairs. Arthur and Martha made their way up the side stairs, with the goose not far behind them. Tristan, eternally gentle, arrived a few minutes later carrying tea and biscuits he had never been asked to bring, and no one ever really knew where he had made them.

Arthur turned to Martha. "I will show you how coaching works. Watch closely."

Tristan smiled softly. "Hello! How may I be of assistance today?"

Martha whispered, "Oh good. This one won't cry."

Arthur gestured. "Tristan, what is a goal you wish to achieve this week?"

Tristan thought. "Well... I would like to feel more confident speaking during the knight meetings."

Arthur nodded. "That is your Goal. What is the Reality of that right now?"

Tristan blushed. "I... mostly stand behind the pillars."

Arthur kept his tone gentle. "So, what Options do you have?"

"Oh! Maybe... practise saying small things, ask a question, or sit around the table?"

Arthur concluded, "And what exactly Will you commit to this week?"

Tristan inhaled. "I will sit around the table instead of standing behind the pillars."

Arthur beamed. "That is coaching," he said, turning to Martha.

Martha stared at him. "That's it? Just... asking questions?"

Arthur nodded. "Yes. Coaching is not always about telling people how to do things. It is helping people to think and learn for themselves."

Martha stared blankly. "Why?"

Arthur inhaled. "Because when they think for themselves, they take ownership of the action."

Martha blinked, then closed her eyes and shook her head. "That sounds... exhausting."

Arthur folded his arms. "Your turn."

"Oh no. Not yet. I am not ready."

"Martha, you must practise."

She cringed. "Fine. Who do I try it on?"

Arthur took Martha's hand and led her back down to the kitchen. The goose followed smugly behind them.

In the kitchen, Morag was glaring at a boiling pot. Cissy folded napkins while whispering positive affirmations to herself. And then... Eve emerged from the pantry with flour in her hair, chewing on something that probably should not have been chewed. In fact, it probably should have been discarded weeks ago.

"Try Eve," Arthur said.

Martha gasped. "No! I am not trained for that level of danger!"

"Exactly," Arthur said. "Coaching must work even in chaos."

Eve approached nervously. "Am I... in trouble? This turnip has been in the pantry under the cupboard for a few weeks now and I was a bit peckish."

"No, that is fine," Martha said quickly. "We are going to coach you."

Eve's eyes widened in terror. "Is coaching painful?!"

"No!" said Arthur.

"Will it make me cry?!" she asked, looking sad.

"Probably not," said Martha.

"Will it help me stop running into things?!"

Martha hesitated. "Possibly. Who knows."

Eve whimpered. "I don't like 'possibly'."

Arthur stepped back. "Martha, please lead."

Martha squared her shoulders. "Right. First question. We're going to find your **Goal**."

Eve tensed like a startled deer. "Oh no. I don't have goals. I barely have balance!"

Martha inhaled. "What do you want to improve at work?"

Eve blinked. "Oh! That's easy. I want to stop… accidentally breaking things."

Martha nodded proudly. "There! A Goal!"

Eve grinned. "Oh! I'm good at this. Maybe I can set up a women's football team if I can score goals this quickly!"

Arthur shook his head. "That is not what she meant, and I cannot see women's football taking off until at least the 21ˢᵗ century."

Martha moved on. "Right. **Reality** comes next. Eve, what is currently happening when you touch things?"

Eve panicked. "Oh! I break everything. Not intentionally! Just… by existing, I break it! Yesterday I tripped over air! And last week I knocked over a bucket just by looking at it too long! And once I…"

Martha raised her hands. "Stop, Eve, please! Reality, not autobiography!"

Eve gulped. "Right. Reality is, I am clumsy."

Cissy gasped sympathetically. "That must be so hard for you."

Eve sniffed. "It is! I feel like a baby deer who has been kicked by destiny!"

Martha whispered to Arthur, "She's going all emotional again."

"That's normal," Arthur replied. "Keep her in Adult Mode. Bring her back gently."

Martha straightened. "OK, Eve. **Options**. What could you try to do differently?"

Eve considered. "I could stay still and not move."

"No."

"I could glue or nail my feet to the floor."

"No."

"I could wrap myself in protective bubble wrap."

"Eve, no. That's years before that's invented!"

"I could stop coming to work entirely!"

Martha froze. "Oh dear. That escalated quickly," she said to Arthur.

Arthur leaned in. "This is an emotional hijack. Reset it gently."

Martha placed a hand on Eve's shoulder. "Eve... think of realistic options."

Eve sniffed. "Um… I could practise carrying small things first, ask for help before I pour something heavy, or get Morag to show me better knife techniques so I don't cut myself so often!"

Martha lit up. "Yes! All of these are excellent options!"

Arthur whispered, "Well done."

"Now," Martha said, "what **Will** you do?"

Eve panicked again. "I will, I will, I will…" She dropped to the floor, crawled under the nearest table, and whispered, "I will stay here forever where I cannot break anything."

Cissy rushed over. "*Eve, no!*"

Martha knelt, exasperated. "No, Eve. Coaching isn't about hiding from what you can achieve!"

"I feel safe now though!" Eve squeaked.

Arthur approached. "This," he said calmly, "is a common coaching barrier."

Martha groaned. "I didn't know coaching required crawling under furniture."

Arthur smiled. "Only with Eve."

He knelt. "Eve… what is one small thing you can commit to doing this week?"

Eve hesitated, crawled back out, and whispered, "...I will carry one small bowl of cereal each morning without dropping it."

Martha clapped. "Yes! A GROW plan!"

Eve looked emotional. "You mean... I did it?"

Martha hugged her. "You did."

Cissy hugged them both too. The goose opened its wings, expecting a hug as well.

Morag stared at the scene and muttered, "This is disgusting... but I do love it."

Arthur nodded. "That," he said softly, "is coaching."

Martha stepped away, breathless. "I... coached someone. Properly. Even if she briefly hid under the table."

Arthur smiled proudly. "Yes, Martha. And now... we expand."

"Expand?!"

"Yes. Tomorrow you will learn to develop people's strengths, give feedback, and coach a whole group."

Martha stared at him, pale. "A group? All at once? *Are you trying to kill me?*"

Arthur sighed. "No, Martha. This is coaching, not combat."

Martha narrowed her eyes. "They seem very similar." And with that, she turned tail and headed for her bedroom to lie down.

*****

The sun rose early the next day, and the birds chirped their way through the dawn.

By the time Martha arrived at the Great Hall, she had memorised exactly one sentence of her own coaching wisdom to share with King Arthur: "People will grow faster when you build on their strengths." It sounded clever. It felt clever. But she had absolutely no idea what it meant.

Arthur, of course, was waiting patiently as ever. "Martha," he said warmly, "today we explore how to help people become the best version of themselves."

Martha winced. "The best version? Isn't the regular version exhausting enough?"

Arthur smiled patiently. "No, Martha. When people understand their strengths, they become more confident and more effective. You have seen Belbin's roles. Strengths vary, and that is a good thing."

Martha squinted. "So... instead of shouting at people for being bad at things, I should... praise them for being good at something?"

"Yes. That is part of motivation as well, and coaching can be very motivational."

"But what if they're really not good at anything? Some people are just useless."

Arthur gave her a meaningful look. "Everyone is good at something."

Martha folded her arms. "I will believe that when I see it."

Arthur asked her to list the strengths of her main team members.

Martha looked at the kitchen crew standing in a line. Martha pointed to Cissy. "Cissy's strength is… crying? Is that an actual strength?"

Cissy burst into tears.

Arthur sighed. "Compassion, Martha. Cissy senses emotional shifts quickly. That can be valuable."

Martha blinked. "Oh! Right. Empathy. That is better than her crying." She pointed to Morag. "Morag's strength is yelling." Morag cracked her knuckles and grinned proudly.

Arthur shook his head. "No, Martha. Her real strength is driving action. She gets things moving."

Martha raised her brows. "Even when things don't want to move."

Morag nodded agreeably. "That's usually when I push harder."

Arthur moved on. "And Eve?"

Martha grimaced. "Eve's strength is… chaos?"

Eve perked up. "Is chaos a strength?!"

Arthur coughed. "In Eve's case… creativity. Often unpredictable, but useful in innovation."

Eve beamed. "I am creative chaos!"

Alice whispered, "That sounds worrying."

Finally, Martha looked at Alice. Martha thought. "Alice is… extremely… enthusiastic."

Alice brightened. "Oh! Thank you!"

"And overwhelmed," Martha added.

Alice deflated.

Arthur intervened. "Her strength is eagerness and the ability to learn fast under guidance."

Alice lit up again. "I can learn fast! Once I stop panicking!"

Martha nodded. "Right. Yes," she paused, "so… what is her strength?"

Arthur smiled. "Courage. Resilience. And caring more than you realise."

Martha cringed as if she had been slapped with affection. "Ugh. Feelings."

Arthur raised the sword again. A glowing three-step structure appeared:

Martha stared. "That's it? Three steps?"

"Yes."

"But can I still say, 'What were you thinking?'!"

"No."

"Not even once?"

"No, Martha."

She pouted. "I hate growth."

Arthur turned to Cissy. "Cissy," he said softly, "Situation: yesterday, during the GOAL setting incident... Behaviour: you comforted Eve when she panicked...

Impact: and that helped her feel safe to return to the conversation."

Cissy stopped crying and dried her eyes. "So, I am useful!"

Martha whispered, "Well, that worked too well."

Arthur smiled at her. "Now you try."

Martha's eyes widened. "With anyone?"

"Yes."

"Even Morag?"

Arthur hesitated. "Maybe… not Morag first."

Morag scowled. "I heard that."

Martha turned to Eve. "Eve, Situation: yesterday, during your coaching session… Behaviour: you answered weird things and hid under a table… Impact: which made the whole experience extremely stressful for me."

Arthur leaned in. "Too harsh, Martha."

She sighed. "Fine. Again."

She tried again, softer. "Situation: yesterday, when I coached you… Behaviour: you kept trying, even when you panicked… Impact: you carried on and that showed real bravery."

Eve's eyes widened. "Oh… that was so nice." She hugged Martha so tightly.

Martha wheezed. "Eve! Let go! I cannot breathe. You are squashing my lungs!"

Martha turned to Alice next…. "Alice. Situation: during the stew problem… Behaviour: you stepped in to help Eve… Impact: and it stopped the situation turning catastrophic."

Alice smiled. "You mean… I helped stop the emotional explosion?"

Martha nodded. "Yes. And neither of you dropped a thing."

Alice beamed. "That's the nicest thing anyone has ever said to me."

Martha turned towards Morag.

Arthur whispered, "Be careful."

Martha nodded. "Right. Morag. Situation: the other day, during conflict resolution… Behaviour: you did not punch anyone… Impact: and that was extremely encouraging."

Morag grunted. "I am working on restraint with my therapist."

Alice whispered, "I await the day she fully develops it."

Martha exhaled. "OK. Now that you all know your strengths... we're going to do a small group coaching circle."

Arthur froze. "Martha, are you sure?"

But it was too late. She clapped her hands. "Everyone, sit in a circle!"

They all obeyed. Even the goose joined. Martha stood at the centre. "We're doing group GROW. We start with the Goal. What does everyone want to improve?"

The room exploded.

Eve said, "I want to stop breaking things!"

Alice said, "I don't want to feel overwhelmed!"

Morag said, "I want everyone to stop crying!"

Cissy said, "I want confidence!"

Goose said "Honk!"

Martha raised both hands like a conductor trying to quiet an unskilled orchestra. "One at a time. For me to give good leadership and coaching, I need order."

Arthur whispered to himself, "Good leadership is also knowing when not to run group coaching..."

Martha pointed at Cissy. "You are first."

Cissy wiped her eyes. "My Goal... is to feel more confident."

"Reality?" Martha asked.

Cissy sniffed. "I cry when anyone looks at me."

Alice nodded sympathetically. "I cry when I look at myself!"

Morag rolled her eyes. "Babies."

Arthur leaned to Martha. "Guide them carefully."

Martha continued. "Options?"

Cissy thought. "I could... practise speaking more, try breathing exercises, or Morag could stop intimidating me."

Morag gasped indignantly. "I am not intimidating."

Everyone stared at her.

"OK," Morag admitted. "Maybe I am. Just a little bit. But it is only because I care."

Cissy smiled weakly. "That helps."

Martha nodded. "And what will you do this week?"

Cissy took a deep breath. "I will speak up at least once in the next meeting, even if my voice shakes."

Eve clapped. Alice clapped. The goose honked triumphantly.

Next was Eve. "My Goal is to stop breaking things!"

Martha nodded. "Yes. Reality?"

"I break things."

"Options?"

"I could... move more slowly, ask for help, practise with safer things, wear mittens, glue things down, hold nothing ever again..."

Martha pinched her nose, a habit she had picked up from Arthur. "Pick one option."

Eve nodded. "I will practise moving more slowly."

Everyone applauded. The goose honked, as if approving her new 'slow goose' philosophy.

Then Alice. "My Goal is to stop getting overwhelmed."

"Reality?" Martha asked.

Alice immediately spiralled. "I am overwhelmed right now! I have so many feelings! I don't know what to do with them!"

Cissy comforted her. "It is OK!"

Morag offered her a napkin aggressively.

Arthur whispered to Martha, "Guide her. Ask her a question."

Martha nodded. "What Options could you try right now?"

Alice sniffed. "I could... pause, breathe, ask for help instead of panicking, or use positive affirmations like I do sometimes."

"Which will you do?" Martha asked.

Alice took a breath. "I will pause for five seconds before I react, especially when I feel panic coming."

Martha nodded proudly. "That's growth."

As everyone shared, the energy grew lighter. People laughed, cried, hugged, and supported each other. Morag looked violently uncomfortable with the affection, but tolerated it admirably. Even Arthur seemed moved.

When the session ended, Martha wiped sweat from her brow. "That was... so many feelings. I am emotionally drained."

Arthur rested a hand on her shoulder. "You facilitated growth. Not through force, but through questions, strengths, and feedback."

Martha blinked. "So... this is coaching?"

Arthur nodded. "Yes. This is coaching."

Martha looked around at her team; calmer, smiling, supported. And she whispered, "...I think I like it."

Arthur beamed. "Good, because soon you will require everything you've learned."

Martha paled. "Oh no... what's coming next?"

Arthur answered with dramatic flair. "A real coaching challenge. Someone in Camelot will need help in the morning around breakfast time, and only you can guide them. Be ready."

Martha groaned. "I knew there was a catch."

*****

The next day, the sun rose early to silence. For the first time in a very long time, Camelot was extremely quiet. Not peaceful, just temporarily not exploding. Martha took this as an omen of doom as she scooped her breakfast yoghurt from her pot. Whenever things went suspiciously well in Camelot, something catastrophic tended to follow. A pattern she had begun to recognise. And right on schedule, Arthur appeared in his dressing gown and slippers. He wasn't panicked. He wasn't running. He wasn't shouting. This was even worse. "Martha," he said softly, "we have a big problem."

She dropped her spoon. "I knew it!"

"Follow me," he said, and led her towards the training yard.

There, alone in the middle of the yard, sat Percival, clutching rotas and scheduling scrolls, staring blankly into space.

Martha frowned. "Did someone die?"

"No," Arthur said. "But Percival's spirit is... brutally bruised."

She blinked. "Did Morag punch him?"

"No." Arthur sighed. "He has lost his confidence."

Martha's eyes widened. "Percival?! But he loves confidence! He alphabetises confidence!"

Arthur nodded gravely. "Yes, and today he discovered his new weekly rota, which he spent all night crafting, accidentally scheduled every knight for:
- Two training sessions at the same time
- Lunch before breakfast
- Patrol duty while they were asleep

Martha winced. "Oh no... a scheduling disaster."

Arthur whispered, "He needs coaching, Martha. Not fixing. Not lecturing. Not forcing."

Martha gulped. "You mean... actual coaching? The really deep-dive kind?"

"Yes."

She immediately panicked. "But he is a knight. They shout at people. They have emotions shaped like swords and are happy to use them on anyone."

Arthur placed his hands on her shoulders. "Martha… you have coached Eve. You have coached Alice. You have coached an entire room of emotional tornadoes. You can coach Percival."

Martha stood tall. "…Fine. But if he starts crying, I am leaving." Martha walked across the training yard towards a broken Percival. Percival did not look up. His scrolls fluttered sadly around him like abandoned dreams. Martha sat down beside him. "Percival… why are you… on the floor?"

He whispered, "I have failed the schedule."

Martha blinked. "Is that all? I failed three things before breakfast and never finished my yoghurt."

He did not laugh. He did not move. He simply stared into the void. "I am supposed to be a Chair, the one who co-ordinates, who organises. I am the structure-bringer. And I have single-handedly ruined the week." He whispered dramatically, "What am I… if I am not the schedule?"

Martha swallowed. This was serious. Arthur's voice echoed faintly 'people grow when someone helps them rediscover their strengths'. She nodded to herself. Time for GROW. For real. Martha sat a little straighter beside him, as if posture alone could create authority. "Percival," she said gently, "I am going to ask you some questions. The special kind. The coaching kind."

Percival sniffed. "I deserve no questions. Only pity."

Martha sighed. "Just answer them, you dramatic spreadsheet."

Percival blinked. "...OK."

## G – *Goal*

"What do you want to achieve, Percival?"

He hesitated. "To... get my confidence back. To feel competent again. To... not fear the schedule."

Martha nodded. "Good. That is clear and very reasonable."

Percival added, "Also, I want the knights to respect my work again."

Martha nodded again. "Even better. That is a solid goal."

## R – *Reality*

"Tell me what's actually happening right now."

Percival took a shaky breath. "The reality is... I made one mistake. A big mistake. And now I think I am a terrible person. And I am afraid they will replace me with someone who... doesn't love rotas as deeply as I do."

Martha raised an eyebrow. "Percival, you are the only person in Camelot who enjoys planning, documenting, and colour-coding."

"You really think so?"

Martha stared. "Yes. Literally no one else understands the schedules and calendars."

He nodded slowly. "That is… so true."

"And your one mistake did not hurt anyone," she said gently.

He nodded again. "…also, very true."

## O – *Options*

"What could you do now to rebuild your confidence and get the other knights to respect your work again?"

Percival thought. "I could… talk to the knights. Apologise." He grimaced. "That's terrifying."

Martha nodded. "What else?"

"I could… simplify the rota. Use fewer colours. Maybe… fewer fonts. Less italics."

"What else?"

Percival hesitated. "I could… ask for help. But… that feels like failure."

Martha shook her head. "Percival. Asking for help is not failure. Asking for help is the right thing to do when you feel overwhelmed."

He stared at her as if she had said something profound. "You make it sound... helpful."

"It is helpful."

He hesitated. "Then... I suppose... I could ask for support in redesigning the rota."

Martha beamed. "There you go."

# W – *Will*

"What will you do after our session?"

Percival inhaled deeply. "I will... talk to the knights."

Martha nodded. "And?"

"I will... revise the rota with their help."

"And?"

"...I will stop assuming one mistake makes me worthless."

Martha froze. "That... is a good one, Percival."

He wasn't finished. "And... I will accept that my strengths are not perfection. They are foundations to grow on."

Arthur, watching from a distance, smiled. Percival wasn't spiralling. He was learning.

Martha remembered the next tool. "Percival, may I give you some feedback now?"

He nodded nervously.

Martha delivered her best SBI yet. "Situation: this morning, when I saw you upset in the training yard... Behaviour: you were open and honest about your feelings... Impact: that allowed us to work through this together. It shows courage."

Percival's eyes shimmered. "You... you think I am courageous?"

Martha nodded. "Yes. Vulnerability is courageous. Even for knights."

He wiped a tear. "So, I am still... me?"

Martha smiled. "Yes. You are still Percival, Master of Rotas, Keeper of Calendars, Protector of Time Slots."

Percival gasped. "That's the nicest title I have ever heard."

Martha pointed to his scrolls. "Percival... your strength isn't perfection. It is organisation, care, dedication, and the way you help others know where to be."

Percival straightened proudly. "You're right. Camelot needs me."

"Yes," Martha said. "And more importantly... Camelot needs you to be OK with being human."

He blinked. "That… might take practice."

"Yes," she said kindly. "And I can coach you."

Percival smiled for the first time in a long time. With newfound bravery, Percival gathered the rest of the knights. "I have an announcement," he declared.

The knights leaned in.

He steadied himself. "I made a mistake. But I am revising the schedule now, and I would appreciate your input."

The knights froze. They were not used to knights expressing vulnerability.

Gawain muttered, "I… I don't know how to respond to this. Is this normal?"

Tristan stepped forward gently. "I'd be happy to help, Percival. Anyone for a brew?"

Lancelot smiled. "And I shall provide emotional support… and hair styling tips."

Percival stood taller than ever before.

The team came together, truly together, in a way that displayed everything Martha had just facilitated.

Arthur lifted Excalibur to close the lesson. The ruby projector illuminated:

"I... I actually coached people properly," Martha said, full of pride.

Arthur nodded. "You did. And not just anyone either, Percival. A real knight."

Martha exhaled. "Well. That one was exhausting compared to Eve and Cissy. Can I have a week off?"

Arthur shook his head slowly. "No, Martha. Because next time... we tackle Change Management."

Martha let out a long, slow groan. "Why can't Camelot stay the same?!"

Arthur patted her shoulder. "Because if it did... nothing would ever grow or improve."

# CHAPTER NINE

## Change Is Inevitable. Panic Is Optional
### Change Management

Martha had barely sat down at the Square Table with her morning tea and toast when Arthur appeared with a look that suggested he was about to ruin her entire day once again.

He often looked like that lately, but this time it was particularly pronounced. "Martha," he said gently, "I need your help with something important."

She clutched her cup like a lifeline. "Is it coaching again? Because I only just recovered from that."

Arthur shook his head. "No. Something bigger. Something that affects the whole kingdom. Something we must shepherd very carefully."

Martha's eyes narrowed. There were very few phrases she feared more than 'major' and 'change' together in one sentence, especially when placed next to each other.

"Arthur," she whispered, "I am very tired. Can we not do that today?"

He sighed. "I am afraid the change is necessary."

She stared at him, inhaled slowly, and stood up with her hands on her hips. "I refuse. Change is terrible. Change causes panic. Change makes people cry. Change breaks things. Change…"

Arthur placed a calm hand on her arm. "…can be exciting," he said, finishing her sentence. "You have just precisely demonstrated why we need to learn about change management."

She sank back into her chair. "Fine. What sort of change?"

Arthur took a breath. "The southern towns are merging their trade routes. It means new systems, new responsibilities, and new expectations for Camelot."

Martha blinked. "That sounds… complicated."

"It is," he said through gritted teeth.

"And exhausting," she added, putting a hand to her brow.

"Yes. It will be," Arthur confirmed.

"And very likely to end in disaster," she concluded.

Arthur nodded. "Only if poorly managed. Which is why we must manage it well."

She groaned softly. "I don't like managing people even on a normal day."

Arthur smiled. "And yet you are becoming *very* good at it."

She frowned, unconvinced.

Arthur lifted Excalibur slightly. The ruby glowed, softer this time, as though aware that change was a delicate business. A glowing vision formed in the air, one Martha had never seen before. Unlike the usual energetic swirls and symbols, this one was calm, almost gentle.

"This," Arthur said, "is the model we will begin with. **Lewin**'s Change Framework." The diagram displayed three simple words:

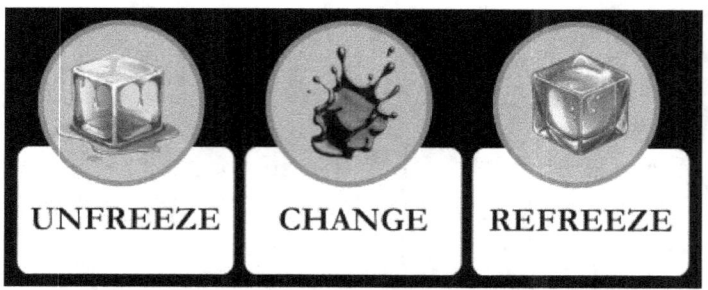

Martha squinted at it. "That looks rather sinister."

"It is not sinister," Arthur assured her. "Kurt Lewin develops this model in 1947 and, put simply, it means people must be prepared before you change something. You cannot drag them into a new way of doing things while they cling to old processes, procedures, or systems."

Martha folded her arms. "Well, I am clinging to the old ways. Firmly."

Arthur nodded. "Yes. That is *exactly* what happens when people close their minds to change and linger in the past." He gestured towards the words. "**Unfreeze** means helping people understand why the current state cannot continue. People must emotionally and mentally loosen their grip on the status quo and come to terms with the need for change."

Martha frowned. "That sounds like persuading people to move out of their comfort zone."

Arthur hesitated. "Well... in the simplest terms, it is."

She pointed accusingly at the words. "I knew it. This is sinister."

Arthur exhaled slowly. "It is honesty. Change without preparation leads to fear, resistance, sabotage, and one day 'fake news'."

Martha sighed. "So, unfreeze means raising people's awareness?"

"Exactly. While showing empathy and communicating truthfully."

She nodded reluctantly. "Fine. I can do empathy. I have some left over from last week."

He smiled faintly. "Good. Today's lesson will require all of it. Come, let us go outside."

They walked to the town square, where the morning bustle was underway. Merchants unloaded crates. Knights purchased armour. Villagers swept pathways. Gardeners sold their wares. Everything seemed strangely normal.

Arthur watched quietly. "Do you see this?"

Martha gestured at the scene. "I see calm. Which is suspicious."

Arthur nodded. "This calm is exactly what will be disrupted by change. And if we do not prepare them, the disruption will overwhelm them."

She considered this carefully. "So, unfreeze means... gently warn them?"

"Yes. Involve them. Give context. Help them feel part of the process."

Martha shuddered. "People are so emotional."

Arthur nodded sympathetically. "Yes. Which is why change cannot be imposed without support."

She stared at him. "And I am supposed to help with this?"

"You must. The change touches every part of Camelot: markets, schedules, deliveries, patrols, and even the kitchen."

"The kitchen?" she said sharply.

"Yes."

She gasped. "Arthur, why didn't you say that sooner? You should have opened with the kitchen. That is critical information."

He waited patiently as she paced.

Suddenly she stopped. "Oh no. The cooks will melt down. Eve will panic. Alice will panic. Morag will break a wall. Cissy will cry. The goose will run in circles. The goat will do whatever the goat does. And I will be stuck in the middle."

Arthur nodded gravely. "Which is why you must help them through the change."

She slumped onto a bench and buried her head in her hands. After a moment, she looked up. "So... how do I prepare them? What do I say?"

Arthur smiled gently. "You use empathy, clarity, and timing. And before anything else *you listen*."

"Listen to what?"

"To their fears, questions, worries, and resistance."

Martha shook her head. "No. That sounds like counselling."

Arthur laughed. "Change management and counselling have a lot in common."

Martha stared at him. "But I am a cook. Not a therapist."

"And yet," Arthur said softly, "you have handled conflict, coaching, communication, and emotions. You know more than you think."

She swallowed. "Fine. Show me what comes next."

Arthur raised the sword again. The ruby displayed a squiggly line with labels:

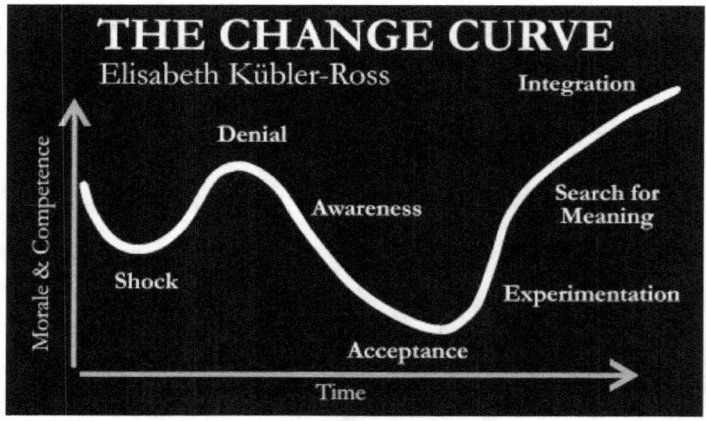

Martha's eyes widened. "That's a lot of feelings."

"You have them," Arthur said gently. "Everyone does. This model helps people understand the emotional journey of change."

She held out her shaking hand. "I am already in shock."

He placed his hand over hers. "When people go through change, they move through stages before acceptance."

Martha leaned in, intrigued. "So, when Eve panics, that might be shock?"

"Yes."

"And when Morag mutters aggressively?"

"Searching for meaning."

"And when Alice cries into a bucket?"

"Denial into awareness."

"And when Cissy tries something new but doubts herself… that's experimentation?"

Arthur nodded proudly. "You, see? You are already understanding this."

She blinked. "Yes. I suppose… I do, only a little bit though."

He looked at her gently. "You have watched your team change. Grow. Learn. You have supported them through conflict and development. You know this curve; it is etched in your bones."

She looked away, slightly embarrassed. "Fine. I might understand it, as I said just a little."

He placed a hand on her shoulder. "You understand it enough to help Camelot."

She inhaled sharply. "No pressure, then."

"Quite a lot of pressure, actually," Arthur said with a smile, "but I have faith in you."

She groaned quietly. "I need more breakfast before faith."

Arthur nodded, stood and they both went for a quick bite to eat a new local street food inspired, pop-up kitchen. After a wonderful smoked salmon and avocado bagel which was lightly toasted and covered with sesame seeds, Arthur turned to Martha. "Come. It is time to begin. We must meet with the senior villagers and knights. They must hear about the change from someone they trust."

She gasped. "You mean you."

Arthur hesitated. "Actually… I meant you."

She stared at him. "No."

"Yes."

"No."

"Yes, Martha."

She shook her head vigorously. "Arthur, I barely understand the changes I am going through myself at my age."

"That," he replied warmly, "is what makes you perfect. You understand what it is like to feel unsure. To feel overwhelmed. To adapt slowly. You will speak with empathy and realism."

Martha slumped. "I will speak with panic and use all the wrong words."

"You will speak with honesty," he corrected. "And they will trust you."

She sighed deeply. "Fine. But if they shout at me, I am running away."

Arthur smiled. "I will not let them shout."

She paused. "Because you'll intervene?"

"Because you will unfreeze them in the right way."

She groaned dramatically and followed him toward the hall.

The Great Hall was already full when Martha arrived. Knights, villagers, gardeners, merchants, and cooks packed the space around the Round Table, all murmuring with the low hum of people who sensed something unsettling was about to happen.

Martha's stomach tightened. She had not un-frozen anyone in her life. She wasn't sure that she should ever be put in charge of thawing out trout from the ice pits, let alone an entire kingdom's emotional state.

Arthur stood behind her, steady and reassuring. "Remember," he whispered, "the goal is not to explain the change. The goal is to prepare their minds for the possibility of change."

"That sounds like manipulation," she muttered.

"It is not manipulation," he said kindly. "It is leadership."

She eyed the crowd uneasily. "Manipulating Leadership!" she said under her breath.

"Are you ready" Arthur said encouragingly.

"Fine. But if this turns into shouting match, I am hiding under a table again. It always works for Eve."

Arthur pushed her gently forward.

The hall quietened.

Martha swallowed. "Good morning," she began, as her voice came out more like the squeak of a cornered mouse than a leader. There was a polite murmur in reply. She continued, "I, uh… have something to tell you. Something important. Something that might be a little… unsettling."

The murmuring rose a little, like a pot boiling.

Arthur nodded from behind her.

Martha straightened slightly. "Camelot will soon be changing its trade and travel systems."

The murmuring erupted fully into whispers and gasps.

Someone dropped a cup. Someone else muttered dramatically, "Here we go again."

Martha raised her hands instinctively. "It is not happening today," she said quickly. "And nothing is final yet. We just… need to prepare ourselves for the idea of it. That's all."

A knight frowned. "Prepare ourselves how?"

A villager added, "And prepare for what?"

A gardener whispered, "Do the vegetables know? Or do we keep it a secret from them?"

Martha blinked. "No… the vegetables don't need to know for now."

"So, we are keeping secrets from them then, what other secrets are we keeping?" he asked with an air of suspicion.

Martha realising her mistake quickly replied. "There are no secrets, none whatsoever, but we need to inform people like yourselves first and we would ask you to pass on the message to the vegetables, when the time comes for them to know accordingly."

Morag, arms folded, asked bluntly, "Why should we change anything at all?"

This was the question Arthur had warned her about. She inhaled slowly, recalling the first step of change: unfreeze.

"Because" she said, "the world around Camelot is changing. Trade is shifting. People want faster deliveries at prime times. Other towns are merging their markets. And if Camelot doesn't adapt… we may fall behind."

There was a thoughtful silence, followed by a predictable ripple of panic.

"Fall behind?" said Lancelot

"Lose trade?" said a market stall holder.

"That sounds dangerous." said Eve. "I like a bit of danger."

"I knew this would happen." said Guinevere

"WILL THE GEESE REVOLT?" shouted a villager extremely loudly.

Martha raised her voice slightly, but not harshly. "I know it feels frightening. I feel frightened too, if I am being honest."

That caught their attention. Martha rarely admitted fear. She usually barrelled through it with stubbornness or denial. But now, she stood openly vulnerable in front of the entire hall.

"It is normal to feel uncertain," she continued. "And annoyed. And worried. All those feelings are part of change. But it doesn't mean the change will be bad. It means we care about what happens for the future of Camelot."

Arthur nodded behind her, quietly pleased.

Cissy raised her hand hesitantly. "Does this mean our work will change? Because… I don't handle sudden changes well. I like to know what's coming."

Martha nodded gently. "And that's why we're talking about it now instead of announcing everything at once. Change doesn't work when it drops on your head like a falling cabbage."

A villager whispered to another, "She has a point. I once suffered a falling cabbage. Never saw it coming."

Martha turned toward the knights. "Percival has helped prepare a draft of what the schedule might look like. It is not final. It is just a starting point. And we want your input."

Percival stepped forward nervously but proudly. His scroll trembled only slightly.

Morag squinted at him. "Is it colour-coded with different fonts?"

He hesitated. "Less than usual."

The crowd murmured approvingly.

Martha took a breath. "This isn't about forcing change. It is about involving you in it. We want to know what you think. What you fear. And what you hope for."

A merchant folded his arms. "What if we don't hope for anything?"

Martha nodded. "Then tell us that too. Every feeling is valid during change."

Even Arthur gave her a look of impressed surprise.

"So," Martha said, "before we go further, I want to listen. Truly listen. What are your biggest concerns?"

The hall went quiet. Then, gradually, hands rose.

A merchant asked, "Will new routes affect travel times?"

A villager wondered, "Will my market stall move?"

A knight asked, "Will our patrol duties shift?"

A gardener whispered, "Will there be new soil zones?"

Eve asked loudly, "Does this mean I will have to stop running into walls?"

Alice turned pale. "Will I have to learn… new things?"

Cissy said softly, "What if I cannot keep up?"

Morag growled, "What if people resist and it all becomes chaos?"

The hall looked to Martha for answers. She instantly wished she had a tapestry nearby to hide behind.

But Arthur gave her a small nod, reminding her of the principles: Acknowledge the fear, Normalise the concern, Reassure the support. "We are not about solutions yet." he said, "Just give support."

Martha steadied her voice.

"All of your concerns make sense. Truly. And every one of you will have questions as things become clearer. But nothing will happen without communication, consultation, and support." She paused. "And no one expects you to handle every part of the change perfectly." Another pause. "Not even me."

That earned a few chuckles.

"And the truth is," she added more quietly, "most change feels overwhelming at the beginning. That's why unfreezing is important. It gives us time to prepare our minds and hearts before anything actually shifts."

A knight asked timidly, "Does unfreezing hurt?"

Martha blinked. "Only emotionally."

Arthur massaged his temples. "What she means," he said diplomatically, "is that unfreezing is simply becoming aware. It opens space for clarity, participation, and choice."

A villager nodded slowly. "Like warming up dough before shaping it."

"Yes," Arthur said. "Exactly."

Martha softened. "So, we will warm up as a kingdom. Together. Gently."

The group seemed to settle at this. Even the goose stopped fussing, which was impressive given the goose fussed at everything and Barnaby returned to the gardens for a munch on some of Guinevere's favourite Peonies.

Arthur stepped forward. "Now we move to the next phase. **Listening**. And capturing concerns. And understanding who needs reassurance, who needs clarity, and who wants involvement."

Cissy raised her hand again. "What do we do if we feel scared later? Or frustrated? Or like Eve, we want to hide under the table?"

Eve nodded vigorously. "Yes, hiding under tables is very soothing."

Martha smiled gently. "Then you come to me. Or to Percival. Or to each other. We're a team. And teams talk and support one another during change. No one has to go through it alone."

There was a tangible shift in the room. Shoulders eased. Postures softened. People exhaled. Some nodded to one another, their concerns now spoken rather than swirling around inside them, causing stress or anxiety.

Arthur leaned in. "Well done," he whispered. "They are thawing."

Martha allowed herself a small smile. "I did not panic. And I did not faint."

"Not once."

"And no shouting."

Arthur hesitated. "Martha, one villager did shout 'Will the geese revolt?' but that's hardly your fault."

She exhaled. "So, what happens next?"

Arthur gave her a look she had learned to dread. "Next," he said, "we handle resistance."

She flinched. "Oh no... not resistance. I have seen resistance. Resistance is where people become unreasonable, emotional, unpredictable, and behave like the world is ending."

Arthur nodded. "Yes, Martha. Resistance is exactly that."

She groaned. "I knew having that extra breakfast bagel was a bad idea."

Resistance did not arrive quietly. It never does.

*****

The morning after the unfreezing meeting, Martha walked into the courtyard ready to take things one step at a time, only to find that Camelot had taken three steps backwards, one sideways, and a spectacular leap into unnecessary distress.

A crowd had formed. Knights on one side. Villagers on the other. Gardeners somewhere in the middle holding rakes like defensive weapons. The goose stood on a barrel again, honking at anyone who dared come close and Arthur stood nearby as she approached.

Martha just stood and stared at the scene in front of her. "Arthur," she murmured, "why does it look like everyone is preparing for war?"

Arthur sighed a long, quiet sigh that suggested he had foreseen this. "This," he said, "is resistance."

"Of course it is," she replied. "Because yesterday they listened politely, and today they're behaving like jelly is raining down upon us."

Arthur nodded sympathetically. "That is the nature of change. At first, people nod. The next day, they panic. The day after that, they accuse you of trying to destroy everything."

She squinted. "Has anyone accused me yet?"

"Give them a minute." He said looking at the imaginary watch that was yet to be invented.

And indeed, not a minute later, a merchant spotted Martha and pointed as if she were a mythical beast. "There she is," he announced, "the one who said we might have to move our market stalls."

"I did not say that!" Martha protested.

The merchant shouted back, "You implied it!"

"I did not imply it!" she said indignantly.

Another villager chimed in, "You breathed suspiciously after saying 'change'!"

Martha threw her hands up. "What does that even mean?"

Arthur placed a calming hand on her shoulder. "This is normal. People often misinterpret uncertainty as a catastrophe."

She stared helplessly. "But we have not even given them the details yet."

"Precisely why they are frightened." he said calmly.

A knight approached. It was Sir Alexander, a rather large, strong man, who currently was looking like someone had stolen his favourite chair. "Martha," he said, "I have concerns."

Martha braced herself. "All right, tell me."

"I heard," Alexander said solemnly, "that the new trade routes will require us to learn mathematics."

Martha blinked. "No one said anything about mathematics Alex."

"That's what I feared," he whispered dramatically.

Arthur cleared his throat. "This," he said softly to Martha, "is exactly the right moment to introduce another model."

She stared at him. "Does the ruby projector ever get a day off?"

"Unfortunately, not," he replied.

He lifted Excalibur. The ruby glowed and displayed a new, simple structure in the air:

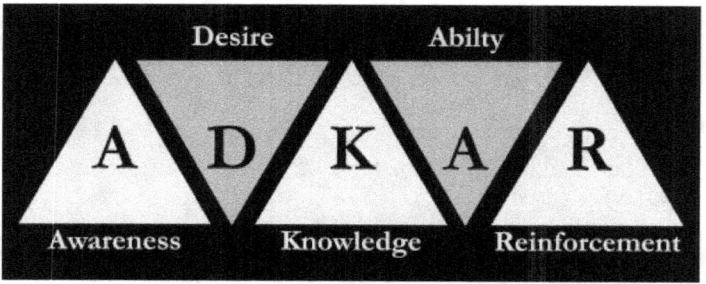

Arthur tapped the glowing words gently. "This makes the mnemonic **ADKAR**," he explained. "It is a model for guiding individuals through change and sits alongside the Kübler-Ross curve, A gentleman by the name of **Jeff Hiatt** will bring this model to the table just before the 21st Century to guide individuals in organisations through successful change."

Martha frowned. "Adkar, sounds more like the name of a sorcerer."

"He is not a sorcerer," Arthur assured her. "It is a sequence that Jeff, will create to give people an **A**wareness of why the change is needed. A **D**esire to participate. The **K**nowledge of how to change. An **A**bility to carry it out. And **R**einforcement to maintain it."

Martha nodded slowly. "So… we've done **Awareness**."

"Yes, we have."

"And now comes **Desire**," she said hesitantly.

Arthur nodded again. "And as you can see… they do not desire it."

Martha gestured wildly at the courtyard, where a heated debate was brewing between a knight and a villager concerning whether trade routes would disrupt the geese's feeding schedules. "How am I supposed to convince them to want to do this?" she asked.

Arthur smiled softly. "Not convince. Understand. Support. Address fears. And find reasons that matter to them."

Martha sighed deeply. "Fine. Tell me where to start."

Arthur gestured toward the crowd. "Start with listening. Again. And do it like a coach. Not like a commander."

She nodded reluctantly. "All right. But if someone blames me for mathematics again, I am leaving."

She stepped into the middle of the courtyard. "Everyone," she called out, "I can see you're concerned. Let us talk through this."

Over half a dozen hands shot into the air. And a dozen voices spoke at once.

"What if prices rise?"

"What if my stall moves?"

"What if the route change brings strangers?"

"What if I have to change my routine?"

"What if my geese will not adapt?"

"What if patrol routes double?"

"What if I become lost on the new map?"

"What if the goat gets confused?"

Martha held up her hand. "One at a time," she said gently. "I promise every single concern will be heard."

The crowd quietened.

Arthur nodded approvingly.

She turned to the merchant who looked the most animated. "You first," she said. "What concerns you most?"

He exhaled. "I like things the way they are," he admitted. "The current system works for me. And change usually means more work, more mistakes, and more confusion."

Martha nodded. "That makes sense. You want stability."

He looked surprised. "Yes. Exactly."

She moved to a villager. "And you Sir?"

The villager shrugged. "I am worried I will not understand the new system. I barely understand the old one."

Martha nodded. "That's fair too. You want clarity."

Another villager added, "I am worried I will lose my place in the market."

She nodded again. "Madam, you want security."

A knight spoke next. "I don't want to learn new patrol routes."

"You want predictability then," she said.

A gardener whispered, "I don't want people trampling over the vegetable borders like they used to."

"So, you want consistency." she said, trying hard to recall all the needs of the people.

And slowly, the entire courtyard calmed, because each person realised their worries were not ridiculous, they were human.

Arthur whispered, "You are helping them to build desire. That is great success towards the second step."

Martha whispered back, "This is exhausting. I deserve a cup of tea and biscuit for this."

Arthur chuckled and from nowhere Tristan arrived with a tray!

Martha took a chocolate digestive and turned to the crowd. "I hear your fears," she said. "You are looking for, stability, clarity, security, predictability and consistency, and none of these things are silly, they are all very important. Change often feels bigger than it actually is, especially when you hear or see only a part of the picture. So, let us fill in some gaps together."

The tension loosened.

She continued, "Most of the changes will not happen all at once. Some will not even affect you. Some of them you will barely notice. And anything that *does* affect you will come with guidance, explanation, and support."

Cissy raised her hand. "Will there be training?"

Martha nodded. "Yes. Of course there will be training sessions, they are vital in any change programme."

A knight asked, "Will there be written instructions?"

Percival stepped forward proudly. "There will be extremely clear written instructions."

Another knight whispered, "Will it be colour-coded, with bold Times New Roman font?"

Percival smiled. "Less than usual and I am enjoying Tahoma currently."

A ripple of relief spread across Camelot.

Arthur leaned in. "That's **Knowledge**. And **Ability** will follow."

Martha smiled. "Everyone will have time to learn," she said. "And we will learn together. No one will be left behind."

She looked at the villagers. "If you're worried about your stalls, we'll review them with you."

She looked at the knights. "If you're worried about patrol adjustments, we will walk you through them slowly."

She looked at the gardeners. "If you're worried about the vegetables... we will respect their space."

Even the gardeners nodded contentedly.

"And I promise," she added softly, "I will not let anyone change things faster than you can handle."

A hush settled.

Then a quiet voice spoke up. "Thank you," someone murmured.

Another added, "That helps."

Someone else said, "I feel better now."

Arthur smiled at Martha. "You've brought them into the change," he said. "That is true leadership at its best."

She allowed herself a small, tired smile. "I think... I might be getting good at this change stuff as well."

"Not might be, you are" Arthur said kindly.

The courtyard gradually dispersed, with lighter hearts and fewer anxious mutterings. Even the goose seemed calmer, which Martha took as a success. She leaned against a pillar, exhaling deeply. "So… is that the end?" she asked hopefully.

Arthur shook his head. "Not quite. There is one final piece."

She groaned softly. "Of course there is."

"*Reinforcement*," Arthur said. "The last step of ADKAR. Ensuring people maintain the new behaviour over time. Supporting them when they slip. Encouraging constant progress."

Martha rubbed her forehead. "Encouraging progress? I am terrible at that."

Arthur smiled warmly. "Not anymore."

She considered that. "So, the unfreezing is done. The change is beginning. And the refreezing is next."

He nodded. "Correct."

"And I… am supposed to help refreeze an entire kingdom."

"You are. And you will not do it alone."

She sighed and nodded. "All right. I will do it, but with whom?"

Arthur placed a hand on her back and guided her gently toward the kitchen. "With me, let us begin planning, and perhaps…." he said.

"And perhaps," she mumbled, "we will begin with tea."

Arthur smiled. "Tea is an essential part of change management."

She smirked. "I knew it."

And as they walked away, the goose followed them, waddling with renewed purpose, as though it too believed the future of Camelot was suddenly manageable.

For the first time, Martha felt that maybe, just maybe, it was.

# CHAPTER TEN

## Martha Without Arthur
Putting It All Into Action

Martha was pruning a row of limp herbs in the kitchen garden when Arthur appeared beside her with an expression she had learned to dread. It was the expression of a man about to entrust her with something she absolutely did not want.

"Martha," he said softly, "I have been summoned."

She dropped her gardening shears into the rosemary. "Summoned? By what? Who? Please tell me it is not a dragon."

"It is not a dragon. It is an alliance meeting at the far border," he continued. "An urgent one. I must leave immediately by horseback."

Martha blinked at him. "Arthur... what happens to Camelot when you leave?"

He gave her a gentle smile that made her stomach drop. "I have already decided. While I am gone, you will serve as Acting Steward."

She stared at him, unblinking. "Arthur. *That* sounds like a terrible idea."

"It is the right idea."

"No. It is *terrible*," she said, shaking her head vigorously.

"You are ready for this, Martha," he said reassuringly.

"I absolutely... am not ready."

He placed a steady hand on her arm. "You have learned communication, decision-making, delegation, conflict resolution, coaching, and change management. You have done brilliantly. You can lead Camelot for the day."

Martha swallowed. "One day?"

"Yes."

"One whole day?"

"Yes."

"Can I sleep through the whole day?"

"No."

She groaned.

Arthur gave her an encouraging nod. "The kingdom trusts you. I trust you. You simply need to guide everyone as I would."

Martha looked horrified. "You mean calmly? And wisely? And without shouting?"

"Yes."

She inhaled sharply. "I can do two of those. Possibly."

Arthur squeezed her hand affectionately. "You will not be alone. Merlin is… somewhere nearby. Guinevere is available if needed. And Percival has updated the rota."

That last part did not reassure her. Before she could protest again, Arthur mounted his horse, gave her a look filled with confidence she did not feel she deserved, and rode out through the castle gates. The horse vanished into the morning mist.

Camelot was hers. She stood very still. A full minute passed. Then she whispered, "Oh no."

The first hour went surprisingly well. Nothing exploded. Cissy hadn't cried. Morag hadn't threatened anyone. Tristan had made tea. Alice hummed positively. Percival read through the rota with only minor shaking. Then, just as Martha was beginning to believe the day might be manageable, a frantic villager came sprinting through the courtyard.

"Acting Steward! Acting Steward! There is a dispute at the southern border."

Martha stiffened. "Oh. Good. Excellent. A border dispute. Perfect for my second hour."

The villager gulped. "They are arguing over ownership of the bridge."

Martha frowned. "Which one?"

"The only one."

She coughed. "That feels important."

"It is," the villager said. "Because the bridge… is closed."

Martha blinked. "Closed?"

"Yes. Someone put up a rope. And a sign on a barrel."

Martha rubbed her forehead. "What does the sign say?"

The villager recited: "No one must cross the bridge. This land beyond it belongs to Vallon's Hill, not Camelot."

Martha stared. "It does not belong to Vallon's Hill."

"I know."

"And yet someone has claimed it."

"Yes."

She pinched the bridge of her nose as Arthur would. "Who is in charge of Vallon's Hill?"

"A man named Cedric."

"Cedric. Of course it is Cedric."

The villager hesitated. "There is also a queue on the M20 of supply wagons stretching back five miles."

Martha inhaled sharply. "What sort of wagons?"

"Food. Grain. Cloth. Tools. Medicine. The usual."

"And they cannot pass?" she asked, with melodramatic despair.

"No."

Martha straightened. Right. This was her job now. "Fetch Percival," she said. "And the knights. And Morag. And Cissy. And Eve. And Alice. And the goose, if it insists."

The goose trotted after them, apparently assuming its presence was mandatory.

The entire group marched to the southern border. Martha had imagined something grand: dramatic flags, guards, but all there was, was a grumpy Cedric standing on a rock making proclamations, plus one small rope, one wooden sign, and one knight trying to reason with him. Behind them, Martha could see at least twenty wagons lined up, their drivers sweating in the sun.

Cedric stood with his arms crossed against his rather portly stomach, chin raised defiantly. He was accompanied by two men dressed in black, who looked bored by the whole thing and not particularly bright.

Kay, who had been negotiating, looked relieved when he saw Martha. "Acting Steward," he said, "thank goodness you're here."

Martha nodded to him, then turned to Cedric. "Hello. My name is Martha. I am acting on behalf of King Arthur. Can you explain why this rope is here?"

Cedric sniffed. "This land is ours."

Martha looked at the land. It looked exactly like every other piece of land in Camelot. "I am very confident it is not," she said.

Cedric squared his shoulders. "I received a letter from our elders stating the boundary lies one tree eastward from where Camelot believes it lies."

Martha looked at the tree. It leaned dramatically, as if trying to escape the argument entirely. "And who sent the letter?" she asked.

Cedric puffed up. "Elder Bran. He wrote: 'The land beyond the tree is Vallon's Hill territory'."

Martha stared at the parchment Cedric handed her. It was written in crayon, which had not yet been invented. She blinked slowly. "Cedric," she said carefully, "this is not a legal document. It appears to have a... very poor drawing of a chicken on it."

Cedric squinted. "The chicken is the official seal of Vallon's Hill."

Martha glanced at the men behind him. Both nodded solemnly. She exhaled. "Fine. Let us set aside the chicken for now. Why is the bridge closed?"

"Because Camelot is violating our border."

"I assure you, we are not."

Cedric pointed dramatically at the bridge. "Your villagers crossed over with bread this morning."

Martha blinked. "Bread?"

"Bread," he repeated.

She stared at him. "It was breakfast."

"Smuggling," Cedric said, with a sniff of conviction.

She pinched her nose again. "Cedric, bread is not contraband."

He sniffed again. "Bread can be anything if handled improperly."

Martha closed her eyes briefly. This was the worst possible day for the kingdom to lose Arthur.

Cedric continued, "Until border ownership is clarified, no goods may pass."

Behind Martha, a wagon driver called out, "The butter and soft cheese is melting!"

Another shouted, "The grain is getting damp from the heat and humidity!"

A third yelled, "My chickens are unionising!"

Martha looked at the endless wagons. She looked at Cedric's rope. She looked at the increasingly distressed goose. She inhaled deeply. This was the moment. The ultimate test of her leadership. She remembered Arthur's teachings:

- Communicate
- Mediate
- Negotiate
- Coach
- Decide

She stepped forward. "Cedric," she said calmly, "I understand you feel your territory is under threat."

Cedric blinked. "I do."

"And you want respect for Vallon's Hill."

"Correct."

"And clarity around the border."

"Yes."

Martha nodded. "And I want those wagons to move before we have a famine."

Cedric's eyes flicked towards the sweating drivers.

Martha lowered her voice. "Let us find a way to do both."

Cedric hesitated.

She added quickly, "Perhaps we should establish joint ownership of the bridge. Temporarily. Until Arthur returns."

Cedric blinked. "Joint ownership?"

"Yes. Shared control. Both kingdoms benefit."

He puffed up slightly. "That would... be respectable, I suppose."

"Excellent," Martha said warmly. "In the meantime, we can form a temporary agreement to let goods pass freely."

Cedric hesitated.

Martha held out her hand. "Cedric... no one wants conflict over a bridge. We just need a loose trade agreement to avoid supply chain disruption and keep everything moving, without more bureaucracy and paperwork. Let us be sensible and bow to common sense."

He looked around. The knights were watching. The villagers were watching. The wagon drivers were watching. Even the goose was watching.

Finally, Cedric clasped her hand. "Agreed."

The rope fell. The wagons rolled forward. Drivers cheered. Martha exhaled. She had negotiated a border dispute. *She, Martha* had resolved a diplomatic conflict without shouting or hiding under a table. She felt both empowered and faint.

Kay approached her. "That was well done."

Martha nodded, feeling strangely proud.

Then another villager ran up, breathless. "Acting Steward," he gasped, "a new problem has emerged."

Martha closed her eyes. "Of course it has."

He continued, "There is an illness spreading in the market. People are calling it the 'Coughing Plague'. They believe it has been spread by dragons."

Martha stared at him. "And what does this illness involve?"

"Coughing," he said, surprised by the question.

"That seems manageable."

"And a small fever," he added.

"Fine."

"And then there is the dramatic fainting."

"Eve does that on Tuesdays."

"And we think," he added nervously, "it spreads very quickly."

Martha felt the ground sway. "Oh no," she whispered.

Arthur had trusted her to lead Camelot for one day, and she had already faced a border dispute, a near supply chain collapse, and now a pandemic. She steadied herself. "I can handle it," she whispered.

The goose honked in agreement.

By the time Martha returned to the castle, the news of the Coughing Plague had travelled faster than any wagon, rumour, or goose gossip. Villagers hurried indoors. Merchants whispered in tight circles. Knights looked suspiciously at anyone who so much as sniffed. Cissy washed her hands seventeen times in a row. Eve wore a bucket on her head as a form of PPE. Alice tucked herself behind the nearest barrel.

Martha pushed through the anxious crowd. "All right. Who is actually ill, and who is panicking?"

It turned out the ratio was not encouraging. A baker sat on a stool, coughing delicately. A young stable hand coughed loudly and dramatically, mainly for attention. Two villagers coughed because they saw the others cough and felt entitled. A knight coughed to test whether he could cough. The goose honked at them all with complete suspicion.

Martha raised her hands. "Stop. We will handle this. But we need information."

She turned to the baker. "When did your cough start?"

"This morning," he said. "I felt fine yesterday. Then suddenly I coughed seven times in a row."

Eve gasped. "Seven is a magical number."

Alice peered round the barrel. "That's how many magic mushrooms I accidentally ate last month."

Morag folded her arms. "It is an illness. Not mushrooms. Not magic ones."

Martha knelt by the baker. "Any fever?"

"Yes. A bit."

"Anyone else in your house ill?"

"The children. And my wife."

Martha nodded. Household spread. That made sense. She turned to the stable hand. "And you?"

He coughed loudly again. "The same."

"Anyone else in the stables ill?"

He hesitated. "…about half of them."

Martha sighed. "Right. This is a real problem."

She needed clarity, consistency and compassion. And, as if Arthur were nearby, a ruby projection shimmered above her:

**In times of crisis, LEADERSHIP is:**
Clarity + Consistency + Compassion

Martha read it twice. "That's... actually very helpful."

Morag grunted. "So, what's the plan?"

Martha stood. "We need to slow the spread, keep people informed, and support those who are ill."

Cissy wrung her hands. "How do we slow the spread?"

Martha thought. "First, we limit gatherings. No big parties. No drinks after work."

The crowd tensed.

"This is not a lockdown," she said quickly, "just fewer large crowds, and more space between people."

Morag nodded. "That makes sense."

Percival raised a trembling hand. "What about the marketplace?"

"We reduce the number of stalls open at any one time. Rotate them. Keep pathways clear so people do not crowd."

Villagers whispered nervously, but not angrily. That was progress.

"And we need hygiene," Martha added. "More washing. More cleaning. More... not touching everything."

Eve raised her bucket-helm. "You can always wear one of these."

"No."

"But mine is very comfortable."

"No."

Alice peered out. "What about people who are sick?"

"We deliver food to them, so they do not have to leave their homes," Martha said. "A schedule. Contact-free."

Cissy brightened. "I can help with that."

"And Morag," Martha added, "you can organise the healthy volunteers."

Morag looked satisfied. "Finally. Something useful."

Percival stepped forward, clutching a scroll. "And I can track who is unwell and who needs support."

"Perfect," Martha said.

She was forming a plan. Not perfect, but workable.

Then a merchant rushed towards her, panting. "Acting Steward! The supply wagons have not moved."

Martha frowned. "I saw them moving when I left Cedric."

"Yes," the merchant said breathlessly, "but at the next border, a different group has claimed half the wagons owe additional tax for crossing the first rope, even though the rope was… unofficial."

Martha stared. "What tax?"

"The rope tax."

"There is no rope tax," she said, in disbelief.

"There is now," he said.

Morag muttered, "A rope-based economy. That's innovative."

Martha pinched the bridge of her nose. "So, the wagons at the second border are stuck."

"Very stuck," the merchant said. "And now the drivers are arguing because no one knows who is allowed to pass, when, or why."

Martha groaned. "So, the border reopened, but the supply chain collapsed anyway."

"Yes."

She looked at Percival. "Is this… familiar?"

Percival nodded slowly. "It appears to be what Arthur once described as 'a structural bottleneck caused by inconsistent agreements and poorly co-ordinated policies and procedures'."

Martha blinked. "Arthur said that?"

"Well… he said, 'This kind of nonsense will happen in the distant future when certain kingdoms leave important alliances without proper planning'."

Martha frowned. "Why would anyone do that? That is stupidity."

Percival shrugged. "Arthur said people in the early 21st century can be difficult to understand."

Martha sighed. "Well, apparently we have invented that nonsense early." She turned to the group. "We need a team focused on the supply chain. Clear roles. Clear communication."

Morag crossed her arms. "I will lead that team."

Martha nodded. "Good. Take Lionel with you. He respects boundaries, supposedly, and will not argue with Cedric."

Morag left with Lionel and several other knights, barking orders before she was even out of earshot. Now Martha had two ongoing crises: illness and supply chain. She needed structure. "Percival," she said, "we are going to use coaching. On the whole kingdom."

He blinked rapidly. "What?"

"I need you to help me clarify goals, reality, options, and next steps for each crisis. Break it down so I don't panic."

Percival nodded earnestly. "Of course."

He unrolled a new scroll. "What is our goal?"

"To keep people safe and fed," Martha said.

"And the reality?"

"Confusing. Fast-moving. People are scared."

"And the options?"

"We manage illness locally, support households, guide the marketplace, co-ordinate hygiene, and fix the supply route."

"And the way forward?"

Martha exhaled. "Group assignments. Regular communication. Calm leadership."

Percival smiled. "That is very good."

Martha lifted her chin. "Right. Let us get to work."

For the next few hours, Martha moved through Camelot like a conductor guiding a panicked but well-meaning orchestra. She helped Cissy organise delivery teams. She helped Morag negotiate with border guards at the second checkpoint. She reassured villagers who feared catching the illness. She encouraged knights to step back when their voices became too loud. She coached Alice into leading the hygiene team. She calmed Eve, who began wearing three buckets stacked together on her head. She explained to merchants that change would not ruin them. She comforted a crying boy who worried the goose was contagious.

All the while, the illness spread slowly but not explosively. People followed hygiene advice. The supply wagons began moving again after Morag persuaded Cedric's cousin not to invent a new 'shadow tax'.

By late afternoon, groups were meeting outdoors at spaced intervals, traders were rotating stalls, knights had created a queue system with spacing, and villagers were delivering food to households, organised gently by Cissy and loudly by Morag.

Martha stepped back. It was messy. Imperfect. Chaotic. But it was working. For the first time in her life, Camelot was functioning not because Arthur told it to, but because she inspired it to.

Percival approached quietly. "Acting Steward, you should know something."

Martha's heart clenched. "What?"

"The merchants asked me to deliver you a message."

"What did they say?"

Percival smiled. "They said thank you."

Martha blinked, unsure she heard him properly.

"And the villagers," he added, "asked if you would continue the daily updates. They said your explanations are reassuring." "And the knights," he added, "said you had more clarity in one afternoon than they usually receive in a week."

Martha flushed. "I… don't know what to do with that."

"Accept it," Percival said.

She looked around. Calmer. Supported. Connected. "Fine," she muttered. "But I still want Arthur to come back."

Percival nodded. "As do we all."

Martha clasped her broom like a sceptre and whispered, "I did it. *I actually led Camelot.*"

The goose waddled up and bumped her leg affectionately, as if agreeing.

\*\*\*\*\*

By evening, Camelot felt different. Not normal. Normal was loud, chaotic, and occasionally on fire. But steadier, as though everyone had collectively realised they were capable of more than they believed that morning.

Martha leaned against a stone pillar, exhaustion settling into her bones. Her legs ached. Her head throbbed. Her apron was streaked with flour, dust, and possibly goose feathers. But she had done it.

Cissy was organising evenly spaced marketplace queues with gentle but firm reminders about distance. Morag was co-ordinating supply wagons so efficiently the drivers looked slightly terrified but deeply grateful. Alice was bravely teaching hand-washing demonstrations using a clean bucket and theatrical enthusiasm. Percival was distributing a simplified rota (in Tahoma) that villagers were actually thanking him for. Even Eve had removed two of her three protective buckets as the coughing began to subside. The goose patrolled proudly, as if ensuring no one violated the new policies.

Martha exhaled. Camelot had changed today… not in structure, but in spirit. Just as she allowed herself a small smile, hoofbeats sounded at the edge of the woods. It was Arthur. He rode in with urgency, dismounted, and took in the scene: villagers working harmoniously, knights following co-ordinated instructions, volunteers delivering food safely, traders rotating stalls, children playing away from crowds. And at the centre, there was Martha: hair wild, apron wrinkled, utterly drained, but quietly triumphant.

Arthur approached her. "Martha," he said gently. "How was your day?"

She stared at him, then said with perfect honesty: "I want a cup of tea and a biscuit, a quick nap, and some silence. And also, I may never lead again."

Arthur smothered a laugh. "Tell me everything."

Martha covered her face. "I am traumatised. I negotiated a border dispute over bread, co-ordinated new supply routes, enforced hygiene because of an illness, coached half the kingdom, and convinced a man named Cedric to lower a rope."

Arthur looked around. "And the illness?"

"Managed," Martha said. "Cissy organised delivery volunteers, Percival tracked cases, Alice taught washing rituals, and Morag glared at the virus until it lost confidence and departed."

Arthur nodded. "And the supplies?"

"Flowing again. Cedric's cousin tried to create a rope tax, then a shadow tax, but Morag explained taxation to him using mildly threatening behaviour. I will need to coach her on that."

Arthur smiled. "And the people?"

Martha hesitated. "They worked together. They adapted. They trusted the process." She paused. "And they trusted me."

Arthur's eyes softened. "They did."

Martha's voice wobbled. "They listened, Arthur. To me. Martha Swainsbucket. I didn't even raise my voice."

Arthur placed a warm hand on her shoulder. "I knew you would succeed."

Martha shook her head. "No. You hoped. That is different."

"Fair enough," Arthur said. "But I hoped very hard."

Martha gave a tired laugh. "Leadership is exhausting."

"Yes," Arthur agreed. "And exhilarating."

"And terrifying."

"Also, true."

"And messy."

"Almost always."

Martha took a slow breath. "Is this what you feel every day?"

Arthur considered it. "Something like it. But I have had years to practise."

Martha looked down at her hands. "And I have had... just ten chapters."

Arthur smiled. "And look how far you've come."

Martha blinked at him. "For the record, I only cried once today."

"That is progress."

"And I didn't hide under any tables."

"Astonishing."

"And I coached people instead of shouting."

"A miracle."

"And I led us through a pandemic crisis."

Arthur's expression softened with pride. "Martha, you did not simply lead through a crisis. You led through multiple concurrent crises. You negotiated, coached, mediated, reassured, taught, co-ordinated, delegated, communicated, and supported your people. You demonstrated adaptability, empathy, courage, and resilience. You were, by every measure, a true leader."

Martha's throat tightened. "Do you really think so?"

Arthur stepped back and lifted Excalibur. The ruby glowed one final time above the kingdom.

A single projection appeared. No diagram, no model, no list. Just one sentence:

> **Leadership is not about command.**
> **It is about lifting others so**
> **they can rise with you.**

Martha stared at it. "That sounds too beautiful to be about me."

"It is entirely about you."

She wiped her eyes before Cissy could see and join in.

Arthur lowered the sword. "There is one final matter," he said. "Your recognition."

Martha blinked rapidly. "Recognition?"

Arthur nodded. "Camelot does not allow leadership to go unnoticed. For extraordinary service during crisis, I hereby name you..." he paused for dramatic effect. "I place upon you the honorary title of... First Steward of the Round Table."

Martha's mouth fell open. "Arthur. No. Absolutely not. You cannot give me a title. I am just a cook."

"You are a leader," he corrected.

"I burn toast," she said, with a schoolgirl giggle.

"And yet you guided a kingdom."

"I shout at people."

"Not today you didn't. In fact, you haven't shouted for many weeks now."

"I don't belong at your Round Table," she said. "I should only be there to polish it."

Arthur's voice softened. "You belong wherever leadership grows."

Martha looked away, flustered. "I don't know what to say."

"You don't have to say anything."

Cissy clapped tearfully. Eve cheered and almost fell into a barrel. Alice burst into joyful sobs. Morag nodded with fierce approval. Percival sniffed into his scroll. Knights, villagers, and gardeners applauded, and the goose honked with gravitas, as though bestowing an ancient honour.

Martha stood still: overwhelmed, proud, terrified, and determined all at once. After a long breath, she whispered, "All right. I will try."

Arthur smiled. "That is all leadership ever asks."

As the sun dipped below the hills, Camelot returned to a steady hum of purposeful activity. Martha stood beside Arthur, watching the kingdom steady itself after a day of upheaval.

She leaned closer. "Arthur… what happens next?"

He looked out across the village lights. "What always happens next. The future."

Martha followed his gaze. "And is the future… difficult?"

Arthur gave a long, knowing smile. "It always is. And it always will be. And it will test us in ways we cannot imagine," he paused, "but the future is also where our greatest work lies."

Martha considered this. "Then I suppose we will lead Camelot towards it."

Arthur nodded. "Together."

The goose honked solemnly, as if sealing the promise.

And with that, the final test was complete.

# EPILOGUE

## The Future, Whether We're Ready Or Not

Camelot was settling into its new rhythm when Arthur approached Martha with the air of someone carrying a secret. He found her in the kitchen, scrubbing a blackened pan with unnecessary ferocity.

"Careful," he said. "That pan cannot have upset you that much!"

She did not look up. "All dirty pans are upsetting me after this week."

Arthur smiled. "Martha," he said gently, "I think you deserve something. Something not just for your leadership, but for your heart."

Her scrubbing slowed. "My heart?" she said suspiciously. "What's wrong with my heart?"

"Nothing is wrong with your heart," Arthur replied. "Quite the opposite. You led Camelot through crisis with bravery, patience, and compassion. You've earned a reward, a personal reward, along with your new title."

She narrowed her eyes. "Is this reward a nap, maybe?"

"No."

"A hot meal without interruptions? That would be nice," she said dreamily.

"Sadly, no."

"A day where Eve doesn't injure herself?"

"That seems... very unlikely."

Martha groaned. "Then what is it?"

Arthur smiled. "A day dedicated entirely to you."

She blinked quickly a few times. "I don't like the sound of that."

"I think you will," Arthur said, motioning to the doorway.

Before she could protest, Cissy, Morag, Eve, Alice, Tristan, and even the goose appeared as though summoned by fate. They stood in a line, beaming with anticipation.

Martha took a step back. "No," she whispered. "Whatever this is, no."

Cissy clapped her hands softly. "Surprise makeover day!"

Martha froze.

Eve bounced into the room. "We have ribbons!" Before falling flat on her face.

Alice held up a small collection of powders and oils, all labelled in enthusiastic handwriting.

Tristan followed in with several dresses over his arm, waving a scroll. "Now, Percival made a schedule. It is colour-coded, and he has moved to using Aptos font this week. And I have some lovely new frocks for you to try."

Morag cracked her knuckles. "I will handle the haircut."

Martha's eyes widened in horror. "You are not cutting my hair."

"I will not cut much," Morag said.

"That is exactly what someone planning to cut too much hair would say."

Arthur placed a reassuring hand on her shoulder. "Everyone wanted to show their appreciation," he said. "This is not about changing who you are. It is about honouring what you've become."

Martha swallowed. "I appreciate the sentiment," she said softly, "but must we involve scissors?"

The group nodded vigorously. "Yes," they said in unison, except the goose, who honked firmly, which Martha assumed meant the same thing.

Cissy took charge first, guiding Martha to a chair in the pantry, which had been transformed into an impromptu beauty salon. An array of colourful fabrics hung from the shelves, lanterns glowed gently, and sunlight streamed through the arched window like soft gold.

Martha sat stiffly, hands gripping her knees. "I don't... do things like this," she whispered.

Cissy smiled warmly. "Today, you do."

Cissy began by brushing Martha's hair with surprising gentleness, humming a tune that immediately soothed everyone nearby. Martha's eyes fluttered closed briefly, only to snap open when Morag approached with scissors, snipping the air like a small dagger.

"Morag," Martha said quickly, "be kind."

Morag raised one eyebrow. "I am always kind."

"No," Martha said. "No, you are not."

Morag shrugged. "Fine. I will be... moderately gentle." She trimmed with surprising restraint, occasionally stepping back with a critical eye before giving the faintest nod of satisfaction. Martha barely felt a thing, so shocking that she had to check Morag's expression for confirmation.

Morag was smiling. A genuine, small, but very rare smile. "You'll look like a commander," she said.

Martha did not know how to respond to that, so she pretended to be deeply interested in a nearby box of buttons.

Next came Eve and Alice, who had been practising facial treatments using vegetable oils and other things they could get their hands on.

"This is cucumber from the gardens," Alice explained, placing cool slices on Martha's cheeks and eyes. "It helps to soothe the skin and reduce puffiness around the eyes."

"And this," Eve added, holding up a carrot, "is for... something. I forgot what. But it feels helpful."

Martha decided not to ask further questions.

Alice mixed oils with delicate care, dabbing Martha's face with a soft cloth. Eve attempted the same, but mostly succeeded in dropping the cloth, apologising nervously, and then trying again with earnest concentration.

Martha found herself smiling. Unevenly, with the lipstick Eve had applied, but sincerely.

Tristan hovered nearby, checking off each step on the scroll and making helpful suggestions like, "Perhaps moisturiser before powder?" which Alice and Eve politely ignored.

Even the goose seemed invested, standing guard to ensure no one spilled anything. After the hair and face came the clothes. Tristan had hand-stitched several garments. They were simple in different colours, but elegant. Martha chose the dress she liked. It was soft blue, trimmed with natural linen, with two deep pockets at the front for "bits and pieces", as she put it. It was practical, comfortable, and flattering in a way Martha had never considered for herself.

"I thought it needed to be something that still felt like you," Tristan said shyly, smoothing the sleeve.

Martha touched the fabric gently. "It is beautiful," she murmured.

Morag nodded approvingly. "And you will not trip on it. I checked."

Eve clapped. "You look like royalty!"

Alice corrected her. "No. She looks like Martha."

Tristan cleared his throat. "The schedule from Percival now suggests we reveal her new look to Arthur."

"Reveal?" Martha repeated, alarmed.

But it was too late. The group guided her from the pantry into the main kitchen area, where Arthur waited with an expectant expression.

Martha stepped forward cautiously.

Arthur's eyes softened immediately.

"Martha," he said quietly, "you look totally radiant."

She froze, then flushed fiercely. "I don't... think anyone has ever said that to me before."

"My words are true," Arthur said with quiet certainty. "Your strength, your kindness, your courage... now all shine on the outside as much as they always have on the inside."

Martha blinked rapidly. "That is... very kind of you to say."

He bowed his head slightly. "It is deserved."

Martha looked at her team. Cissy was beaming. Morag was nodding smugly, while Eve and Alice were grinning from ear to ear.

For the first time in her life, Martha saw herself not as a stressed cook, not as an accidental leader, not as someone stumbling through crisis after crisis, but as someone who was truly valued. Someone important. Someone capable. Someone seen.

She swallowed hard. "Thank you," she whispered, meaning every word.

Arthur stepped forward. "Martha," he said gently, "there is one last thing I must show you. Something not about today, or this year, but about the future Camelot must grow towards."

They walked out into the courtyard. Arthur lifted Excalibur. The ruby glowed for what felt like it really might be the last time.

A projected light came to life in the air: soft, vast, illuminated with 1980s acid pink and neon yellow.

"Martha," Arthur said, "it is time we speak about the future of leadership."

The ruby projection shimmered above the courtyard like a gentle sunrise, casting warm, shifting colours across the sky. Martha still felt a little awkward about the makeover. Appreciative, but awkward, the kind of awkward that made her tug absently at the hem of her sleeve as she prepared herself for whatever Arthur was about to show her.

Arthur stood beside her, expression soft but steady, like someone about to share a truth with the weight of the world on his shoulders. "Are you ready?" Arthur asked.

Martha hesitated. "No," she admitted. "But I suppose I will be if I don't think too hard about it."

Arthur smiled faintly. "That," he said, "is often the entire secret to courage."

She gave a weak smile and braced herself.

The ruby brightened. Shapes formed. Not diagrams. Not words. Not medieval landscapes. But a world unlike anything Camelot could have ever imagined.

Cities reaching the clouds. People of every colour, shape, and voice. Machines gliding across the ground on wheels. Birds made of shining metal soaring through the air. Forests flourishing, shrinking, regrowing. Faces, so many faces, working side by side and sometimes against each other, struggling to understand differences they had never been taught to see.

Martha took a step back. "Arthur," she whispered, "is this real?"

He nodded. "It is a possible future. A future our own world has not yet reached, but is beginning to build. A future where the lessons we teach today will echo louder than we can ever imagine."

Morag muttered, "Looks crowded."

Cissy placed a gentle hand on her arm. "It looks… beautiful."

Alice gasped softly at the flying machines. "Do those giant birds… eat people?"

"No," Arthur said. "They take people where they need to go."

Alice nodded thoughtfully, then whispered, "That is worse."

Arthur raised a hand. "Quiet, all of you. This is important." He looked at Martha. "You have learned every leadership skill I could give you within the bounds of Camelot. But beyond these walls lies a future that will require leaders like you to think beyond comfort, beyond tradition, beyond familiarity."

Martha swallowed. "I barely survived today's makeover."

"And yet," Arthur said, "you continue to lead with compassion, clarity, fairness, and courage. Those are precisely the traits the future will need."

Martha did not look convinced. "Show me, then," she said. "Show me what the future requires."

The ruby pulsed, rearranging the shimmering scenes into three distinct streams of light that twisted together like braids:

Arthur pointed at the first.

## PEOPLE - *Means Diversity & Inclusion*

"The future is not one kind of person. It is all kinds. Leading it will require understanding every voice, not just the loudest ones."

The first stream grew stronger until images filled the courtyard. Martha saw groups of people working together: some in clean offices, some in bustling marketplaces, some in schools, hospitals, workshops. People who looked nothing alike. People who spoke different languages. People whose clothes, shapes, voices, and gestures were unfamiliar. But there was something else. In some places, they were thriving. In others, they looked small, overlooked, pushed aside.

Martha frowned deeply. "What is happening here?"

Arthur spoke quietly. "This is diversity: the natural variety of humanity. And inclusion: the choice to ensure everyone feels they belong."

Martha nodded slowly. "That seems obvious."

"It should be," Arthur replied. "And yet… it often isn't."

The scenes shifted: a skilled woman of colour being ignored in a meeting, a quiet man with brilliant ideas overlooked because he was not confident enough, a person in a wheelchair struggling to enter a building, someone being spoken over because their accent was not clear and another being underestimated because of their young age. And many others whose contributions were dismissed simply because they did not fit the world's expectations, shaped by social media and "*fake news*".

Martha felt a pang of discomfort. "People really do that?" she asked softly.

"They do," Arthur said. "Not always out of cruelty, but out of habit. Sometimes out of fear. Out of learned patterns they never question, patterns that become beliefs and unconscious biases."

Martha looked down at her hands. "I… think I have done that at times."

Arthur's expression was gentle. "We all have. It is a human weakness we must confront. When we acknowledge it, we can learn to change."

The ruby obliged by projecting memories: Martha favouring Morag's advice because Morag spoke with authority, dismissing Alice because she panicked easily, assuming Eve could not handle responsibility, speaking over Cissy without noticing she was even there.

Martha winced. "Oh. That looks terrible. I will never be like that again."

"You are being human," Arthur said kindly. "But leaders notice patterns. And when they do, they change them."

The projection shifted again, showing inclusive workplaces where people thrived: a young apprentice teaching a seasoned craftsperson, a team of different ages, nationalities, and backgrounds solving problems together, a leader making space in a meeting for someone who struggles to speak, a group celebrating differences instead of hiding them.

Arthur gestured towards the images. "The future will need leaders who remove barriers," he said. "Who see ability in every form. Who invite people into circles, not out of obligation, but out of respect. Leaders who question their assumptions, listen with intention, and act with compassion."

Martha's chest tightened. "I want to be that kind of leader."

Arthur smiled. "You already are learning."

The image began to change.

## PLANET - *Means Environmental Sustainability*

"The world you inherit is not your own. It belongs to your children, and their children, and the thousands of children who will come after you."

The second stream widened. Forests filled the projection: lush and green, alive with creatures. Then, gradually, some forests shrank. Rivers clouded. The sky dimmed. Mountains were cut open. Creatures disappeared. Fields became dust.

Martha gasped. "Stop it! Make it stop!"

Arthur waved the scenes away gently, but the feeling lingered like a stone in Martha's stomach. "What happened?" she whispered.

"Neglect," Arthur replied softly. "Short-term thinking. The belief that natural resources are infinite, and human desire is more important than natural balance."

Martha swallowed. "We damage our own world in the future? What madness is that?"

Arthur nodded. "Not always intentionally. Rarely intentionally. But steadily. Quietly. Through small decisions repeated over many generations." He continued, "Future generations will face droughts, floods, fires, shortages, pollution, and loss. Often because leaders become too distracted to notice, focused on winning instead of collaborating."

Martha felt a wave of sadness and shame. "But why? Why would they not care?"

Arthur placed a hand on her shoulder. "They thought someone else would fix it. That someone else knew better. That someone else would stop the damage."

The projection shifted, showing future leaders planting forests, cleaning rivers, reducing waste, restoring ecosystems, and teaching children about the land.

"There is some hope," Arthur said gently. "But only if leaders foster responsibility with accountability."

Martha nodded firmly. "I can help Camelot do better for the future."

Arthur smiled. "And by helping Camelot, you will help the world that grows from it."

Martha hesitated. "What should we do first?"

"Small things," Arthur said. "Simple habits. Sustainable actions. Stewardship begins at home."

"Together?" she asked.

"Always," he said.

The image faded once more, shifting into a new picture.

## PERSPECTIVE - *Means Unconscious Bias*

"The greatest challenge to humanity is noticing our mind's invisible habits."

The third stream brightened. This time, the projection showed reflections, like standing between a thousand mirrors, each slightly tilted. Martha saw herself in every reflection: Confident, yet fearful. Determined, but confused. Fair, while sometimes unfair. Strong, but also vulnerable. Caring, but sometimes distracted.

Arthur spoke softly. "This is the mind's mirror. It shows the hidden assumptions we all carry, assumptions that shape how we perceive others and how we treat them."

Martha frowned. "You mean... the things we believe without knowing we believe them."

"Exactly," he said, sadness in his voice.

She swallowed hard. "Show me mine."

Arthur hesitated, not out of concern, but compassion. "Very well."

The mirrors shifted. They showed: Martha trusting Morag more quickly than Cissy because Morag spoke decisively. Martha assuming Eve was incapable instead of anxious. Martha overlooking Alice's strengths because she panicked. Martha expecting knights to be fearless. Martha expecting villagers to obey quickly. Martha dismissing gardeners as uneducated and lowest in the food chain.

Martha closed her eyes. "Arthur... I feel awful."

"That means you are learning," he said gently.

"But I did not mean to judge them."

"That," Arthur said, "is what makes bias so dangerous. It hides beneath good intentions."

The projection showed people in the future struggling with bias about race, disability, gender, sexual orientation, accent, physical appearance, ability, age, religion, belief, neurodiversity, and experience.

"By the 21st century, they will face challenges we cannot imagine today," Arthur said. "But the roots of those challenges begin here, in every small assumption we make."

Martha's voice trembled. "How do we fix it?"

Arthur's answer appeared, written clearly:

# CARL ROGERS

## Awareness
## Reflection
## Listening
## Correction

The willingness to ask:
What am I not seeing or hearing?
What assumptions am I making?
What changes can I make?

Martha nodded slowly. "I can do that," she whispered. "I want to."

Arthur smiled. "That is the beginning."

Behind them, her team stood silently, each one visibly moved. Cissy wiped tears from both eyes. Alice fidgeted thoughtfully. Eve stared at her hands as if seeing them for the first time. Morag's stern face had softened, ever so slightly.

Arthur turned back to Martha. "You have led Camelot through crisis. But leadership is not measured only in crisis. The future will test us in quieter, subtler ways. The greatest test is how we treat those who are different from us... in voice, in shape, in mind, in experience."

He gestured to the glowing streams of PEOPLE, PLANET, and PERSPECTIVE. "Leadership begins with courage," he said softly. "But it grows with empathy, responsibility, humility, and awareness whilst accepting accountability."

Martha looked at the future visions: overwhelming, beautiful, frightening, hopeful. "I don't know if I am ready," she admitted.

Arthur gave her a warm, certain smile. "You are more ready than you think. And Camelot is ready because of you."

The projection dimmed gently, leaving the twilight sky in its place.

Martha breathed out, long and slow, one hand on her heart as if making an oath. "I will help create a Camelot where everyone belongs," she said with pride. "Where the land is cared for. Where we question every assumption. Where our future and our people can grow safely together in harmony. We will welcome neighbours in trouble or in need. We will not turn people away because they are different. We will learn to love each other's differences and beliefs. We will treat the earth that provides us with food and oxygen with utmost respect. And we will limit our prejudices and work to ensure that future generations understand the dangers of unconscious bias."

Arthur's voice softened. "That, Martha… is the promise of an aspiring leader."

The courtyard fell into a reverent silence. Then a gardener clapped. Then a knight. Then a villager. And soon the whole of Camelot was clapping in the courtyard at the words and promise Martha had spoken. For the first time, Martha felt not just capable or responsible, but ready to step into a world she could help shape.

As the warm evening air settled over Camelot, the kingdom seemed to pause and listen when the clapping had subsided. The shimmering projections of the future had faded into the amber glow of lanterns, leaving only the memory of their lessons suspended between the people gathered around.

Martha stood quietly in the courtyard, hands loosely clasped before her, eyes fixed on the place where the ruby visions had been. For a long moment, she did not speak. She simply breathed, slowly and thoughtfully, trying to absorb the enormity of everything Arthur had shown her. Behind her, the others remained respectfully silent. Morag, arms folded, watched Martha with a depth of respect no one would have expected from the kitchen's most formidable force. Cissy stood with her fingers woven together, her gaze shimmering with pride. Eve clutched her bucket-helmet awkwardly, as though unsure whether the future required protective headgear any more. Alice dabbed at her eyes, and the goose honked softly, a surprising note of solidarity.

Finally, Martha breathed out. "Arthur," she said quietly, "I never thought leadership would look like this."

Arthur stepped beside her, hands clasped behind his back. "Like what?"

She gestured vaguely to the entire kingdom. "Like... listening. And caring. And questioning myself. And learning from people I thought were learning from me."

Arthur nodded. "That," he said, "is the very heart of leadership."

Martha stared at him. "I thought the heart of leadership was telling people to stop running into walls and shouting at one another."

"That is probably part of the first chapter," he replied. "You have completed far more than that."

Martha let out a slow, quiet laugh.

A soft wind curled through the courtyard, rustling leaves across the kitchen garden. The sounds of Camelot preparing for night drifted through the air: soft footsteps heading home, murmured conversations, the distant clatter of dishes as supper was served. It all felt different tonight. Not calmer, not louder... simply more connected. As if the kingdom itself had grown.

Martha looked around. "I don't know if I deserve all this," she said softly.

Arthur shook his head. "Martha, leadership is not about deserving. Leadership is about choosing to step forward again and again, especially on days when you feel unworthy."

She swallowed. "And I suppose these last few weeks... I stepped forward a bit."

Arthur smiled. "More times than anyone could count."

"Martha," Arthur began, his voice carrying gentle authority, "over the weeks you did more than lead Camelot. You taught Camelot how to lead itself."

Martha blushed. "I did not intend to."

"Exactly," Arthur continued. "Leadership is creating a world where others can flourish. Where every voice can speak. Where every person is valued, not for how loudly they shout, but for what they bring to the table, whatever shape that table may be."

A projection reappeared briefly: a single glowing image of the Round Table and the Square Table standing side by side... just as Arthur and Martha were at that moment in time.

"You are the steward of that promise now," Arthur said. "We are not the tables' keepers, but together we are their guardians."

Martha stared at the glowing image. "But... I am just a cook."

"You are a very good cook," Arthur agreed. "And now you are something more."

He let the projection fade. "Tell me," he asked softly, "weeks ago I asked you a question: 'How would you define what a leader is?' How would you answer that question now?"

Martha thought for a moment. She looked at her team. She looked at the knights. She looked at Camelot, the place that had been chaotic, frustrating, overwhelming... but hers. Quietly, she said: "I think leadership is about making sure people don't walk alone."

Arthur's eyes warmed. "That is the lesson leaders spend their whole lives trying to learn," he said. "And you learned it in one sentence."

"I learned it from them," Martha said, gesturing to her team. "I learned it from Camelot." Martha felt something shift in her chest: not pride, not fear, but something deeper. A quiet certainty. A sense of belonging. A sense of stepping into something larger and steadier than she had ever known. She turned to Arthur. "What happens next?"

Arthur smiled gently. "We build," he said. "We improve. We learn. We prepare Camelot for whatever lies ahead."

Martha considered that. "And what lies ahead?"

Arthur looked at the horizon, where the sun was dipping low behind the hills, casting long golden shadows across Camelot.

"The unknown," he said. "And the remarkable."

Martha took a breath. "I can do unknown."

And as the lanterns flickered in the gathering dusk, Martha stepped forward: newly adorned, newly confident, newly aware, towards a Camelot ready to evolve, grow, and become a kingdom of inclusion, sustainability, and fairness. A kingdom shaped not by the might of a king and his knights, but by the heart of a woman who once thought leadership meant shouting in a kitchen and barking orders. She had discovered, instead, that it meant caring for the world and the people within it.

# AUTHOR'S AFTERWORD

*Martha and the Maids of the Square Table* brings together the two crafts I love most: storytelling and leadership development.

Martha and her chaotic Camelot are, of course, fictional. But the lessons she learns are the same ones I have discussed in training rooms from Tokyo to Berlin, and from Hamilton to Riga. The characters around her, however exaggerated for humour and heart, carry threads of real people I have met along the way: the overwhelmed new manager, the quietly capable team member, the confident but mistaken leader, the anxious but willing learner, the practical doer who drives action, and the emotional thinker who notices what others do not.

If you recognise yourself in any of them, or, more likely, in several, that is intentional.

Leadership is not a fixed set of behaviours we perform like the choreography of dance. It is a series of moments, often happening again and again, where we are asked to respond to people, situations, and ourselves with greater awareness, courage, and humanity. It is forever changing because people and generations change. The world of work changes. Cultures change. Expectations change. The most successful leaders are not those who cling to certainty, but those who evolve with curiosity rather than fear.

My hope is that this book leaves you smiling, but also thinking. That it reassures you that leadership, however daunting it can feel, is also joyful, hopeful, and deeply human. I hope Martha's journey helps you see your own with fresh eyes, and reminds you that you are not alone in the moments when leadership feels messy or uncertain.

After nearly forty years in this profession, one belief has remained constant for me:

### *Leadership is not just a title.*

Leadership is a moment in time, again and again, to help others and those around you to find the best in themselves, especially on the days they cannot see it clearly for themselves. And just like Martha, none of us need to walk that journey alone.

# ABOUT THE AUTHOR
## Dale Gunstone

I began my career in Learning and Development when I was barely out of my teens, becoming one of the youngest Leadership and Management Trainers appointed within National Westminster Bank. At the age of 21, I found myself standing in front of leaders who had been in the workforce longer than I had been alive. What I lacked in age, I made up for in curiosity, observation, and an unshakeable belief that people learn best when they feel seen, heard, and understood.

Over the past four decades, I have had the privilege of working across the world, in India, Japan, the United States, the Philippines, Bermuda, and throughout the whole of Europe, from Bulgaria to Spain, Germany to Latvia. Each place offering me a new cultural lens and a different rhythm to leadership. It taught me that leadership is both deeply human and profoundly local, shaped by heritage, community, values, and the unseen norms we carry with us.

I have lectured at university level and continued to design and deliver leadership programmes across diverse industries and cultures. Throughout my career, I have returned again and again to the theories and frameworks that shaped my thinking, McClelland (my personal favourite), Belbin, Lewin, Hersey and Blanchard, Adair, Thomas-Kilmann, Whitmore, Alexander and Fine, De Bono, Kübler-Ross, and many others. These theorists have been steady companions to me and are beneath every conversation, coaching moment, lecture hall, and classroom.

But theory alone has never been enough.

From my earliest days, guided by mentors and colleagues who believed deeply in the power of learning through experience, I learned that leadership truly comes alive through story. Through characters. Through humour. Through recognising ourselves in the mistakes we make, the tensions that surround us, and the quiet triumphs we win. Above all else, I have always been a storyteller, using narrative to help people place theory into the real world.

# THEORIES & SOURCES

The world of leadership and management is rich with frameworks, models, and theories that have shaped how we understand human behaviour at work. This book brings many of those ideas to life through storytelling, humour, and the fictional world of Camelot. The intention has never been to replicate the academic language of the original texts, but to translate their essence into a narrative that helps readers experience, remember, and apply them in everyday practice.

Below is a guide to some of those key thinkers and models referenced throughout the story, for any reader who wishes to explore their fabulous work in greater depth.

## LEADERSHIP AND MOTIVATION

### Hersey and Blanchard – Situational Leadership

Hersey and Blanchard's Situational Leadership model proposes that leaders adapt their approach across four primary styles: directing, coaching, supporting, and delegating based on the development level of the individual or team. Rather than treating everyone the same, leaders learn to respond to what each person needs at that moment.

This concept runs quietly but consistently throughout Martha's journey. Early on, she defaults to directing (often loudly), believing control will bring clarity. As her confidence grows, she begins to coach, asking questions, offering guidance, and encouraging reflection. Later still, she supports her team emotionally, recognising when reassurance matters more than instruction. By the end of the story, she trusts others enough to delegate meaningfully, allowing people to step forward and take ownership.

Hersey and Blanchard's work reinforces one of the book's central messages: leadership is not about authority or consistency of style, but about awareness, flexibility, and respect for human development. Leaders who adjust how they lead create environments where people can grow, and where trust replaces control.

### David C. McClelland – Acquired Needs Theory

The idea that different people are motivated by different dominant needs: Achievement, Affiliation, and Power. This forms the heart of Martha's early leadership lessons. McClelland's work highlights why one-size-fits-all approaches rarely succeed, and why effective leaders tailor their motivation strategies to the individuals they lead.

## COMMUNICATION AND BEHAVIOUR

### Eric Berne – Transactional Analysis

The Parent–Adult–Child model provides a simple and powerful way to understand how people speak, react, and escalate conflict. In Camelot, it explains why some knights shout, why some villagers panic, and why Martha must learn to speak from the "Adult" state.

# ASSERTIVENESS AND BEHAVIOUR STYLES

Although not tied to a single author, the behavioural continuum (passive, assertive, aggressive, responsive) appears throughout the book. It underpins many real-world leadership development programmes by illustrating how different communication styles affect relationships and outcomes.

# TEAM DYNAMICS

## Dr Meredith Belbin – Belbin Team Roles

The nine roles identified by Belbin such as Plant, Shaper, Co-ordinator, Implementer, and Completer-Finisher help explain why teams succeed or struggle. Camelot's characters each reflect aspects of these roles, although under different headings to respect the era of Camelot, showing how diversity of strengths creates a balanced, high-performing team.

# PROBLEM-SOLVING AND DECISION-MAKING

## Edward de Bono – Six Thinking Hats

A creative, structured way of approaching decisions from different emotional and logical angles. De Bono's method appears during Camelot's problem-solving chaos, helping the team move from argument to exploration.

## Root Cause Analysis

This includes techniques such as the "Five Whys" and

fishbone (Ishikawa) diagrams (though presented narratively rather than graphically). These tools encourage leaders to look beneath the surface and address underlying causes instead of symptoms.

## CONFLICT AND DIFFICULT CONVERSATIONS

### Thomas–Kilmann Conflict Mode Instrument (TKI)

Developed by Kenneth Thomas and Ralph Kilmann, this model explains five conflict-handling modes: Competing, Accommodating, Avoiding, Compromising, and Collaborating. The knights, naturally, demonstrate several of these with enthusiasm.

### Sharon and Gordon Bower – DESC Script

A practical tool for structuring assertive conversations: Describe, Express, Specify, Consequences. It appears repeatedly as Martha learns to navigate conflict with more structure and less shouting.

## COACHING AND DEVELOPMENT

### Sir John Whitmore and colleagues – The GROW Model

Perhaps the most widely taught coaching model in modern leadership development. GROW (Goal, Reality, Options, Will) shapes several chapters where Martha learns to guide others' thinking rather than solve everything herself.

## Strengths-Based Leadership

Popularised by Gallup and others, the idea that people grow fastest by developing their strengths (rather than fixing weaknesses alone) underpins Martha's development work with her team.

## Feedback (SBI Model)

Situation–Behaviour–Impact is a simple, powerful feedback structure widely used in leadership programmes and organisational coaching, developed by the Center for Creative Leadership.

## CHANGE MANAGEMENT

## Kurt Lewin – Unfreeze, Change, Refreeze

One of the earliest and most enduring models of change, used to explain why change feels uncomfortable and why communication is essential. Martha's "unfreezing" conversations closely mirror Lewin's philosophy.

## Jeff Hiatt (Prosci) – ADKAR

A structured approach to leading people through change. Martha uses ADKAR as she navigates Camelot's border dispute, supply-chain collapse, and pandemic chaos, all metaphors for real-world organisational challenges.

## Elisabeth Kübler-Ross – The Change Curve

Originally developed to explain the stages of grief, Kübler-Ross's model has since become a cornerstone of modern change management. The curve illustrates the predictable emotional journey individuals often take when faced with significant change.

Her work offers leaders a powerful lens to understand why people react as they do during transitions, and why emotional support is just as essential as practical guidance.

## BROADER THEMES

### Environmental Sustainability

Although not tied to a single theorist, the principles reflected in the book align with contemporary sustainability frameworks and stewardship models taught in organisations and universities worldwide.

### Diversity, Inclusion and Equity

Again, this is not attributed to one source, but draws on global contemporary practices and research into belonging, representation, equality of opportunity, and creating inclusive cultures.

### Unconscious Bias

Grounded in psychological research by scholars such as Mahzarin Banaji and Anthony Greenwald, unconscious bias has become central to modern leadership development. It appears in the book as the 'mind's mirror' a gentle way to explore a challenging subject.